Reconceptions
in
Philosophy
and
Other Arts and Sciences

D0169125

Reconceptions

in
Philosophy
and
Other Arts and Sciences

NELSON GOODMAN

CATHERINE Z. ELGIN

HACKETT PUBLISHING COMPANY

Indianapolis / Cambridge

Pablo Picasso, variations on Velázquez, *Las Meninas,* copyright
ARS NY/ SPADEM 1987

This book is printed on acid-free paper, and its binding materials have
been chosen for strength and durability.

For further information, please address
Hackett Publishing Company, Inc.
P.O. Box 44937
Indianapolis, Indiana 46204

Library of Congress Cataloging in Publication Data
Goodman, Nelson
     Reconceptions in philosophy and other arts and sciences / Nelson
Goodman and Catherine Z. Elgin.
        p.   cm.
   Includes indexes.
   ISBN 0-87220-052-3 (alk. paper)
   1. Methodology. 2. Aesthetics. 3. Symbolism.   I. Elgin, Catherine Z.,
   1948–   . II. Title.
   BD241.G65 1988
   101—dc19   87-31339
                                                              CIP

For Israel Scheffler

Indomitable Student
Exacting Philosopher
Firm Friend

Preface

Reconception may be occasioned by a catastrophe, an inspiration, a worry, a query, a mistake. Now that the beginning when there was nothing is long gone, most of the philospher's work is reconception, his making remaking, his creation conversion. But reconception is not confined to correction, and does not always result in replacement; it may yield illuminating and important alternatives to, rather than substitutes for, a standing conception. Nor are concepts and conceptions exclusively linguistic; they may be pictorial, diagrammatic, gestural, kinaesthetic or of any other sort. Musical variations are reconceptions that are neither verbal nor replacements for the original version. Moreover, whether the concepts involved are verbal or not, reconception does not always amount to alteration in what is named or described or otherwise denoted; it may be in what is exemplified or is expressed or is alluded to indirectly. Thus a change in style or even in vocabulary may sometimes effect a significant reconception.

This book proposes some and examines many reconceptions against a philosophical background that has a general theory of symbols as a prominent part. That makes possible comparisons across seemingly impassable barriers between, for example, the arts and the sciences, the verbal and the nonverbal, the affective and the cognitive. Far from obliterating genuine distinctions between such supposed opposites, it provides means for identifying the distinctions between them while recognizing their often overlooked common features and their kindred roles in the overall process of understanding.

When each new topic is considered, the underlying theory— or at least the relevant part of it—has had to be reviewed, not only because the reader cannot be expected to remember all the sometimes rather technical details, but also because, in the context of a new application, the theory itself may require some revision. An inquiry into a particular question often results in reconsideration of the instruments and methods being used and even of the question asked. In this and other ways, our specific studies lead to modifications in theory, approach, attitude; and the book itself thus carries forward a continuing process of reconception.

Part One surveys the stage this process had reached when work on the present book began. Part Two reports on our recent and current examinations of a wide variety of cases and aspects of reconception. Part Three asks after the more general consequences and purport of all this and, perhaps rashly, suggests supplanting or supplementing some of the most basic and cherished concepts of traditional philosophy.

Most of this book is new. Earlier versions of Chapters II, III, and VII have appeared in journals but no versions of other chapters are now available elsewhere, although versions of some chapters (but not VIII) are in process of publication in one language or another in various collections. Details are given on pp. 167–168.

The book is a product of collaboration; developed, intensively discussed, and fully subscribed to by the two authors. The names at the ends of the chapters indicate only primary responsibility for putting these chapters in shape and are by no means in the interest of what just now is actively discussed as 'deniability'.

We have intruded into many fields—architecture, music, literary theory, etc.—where our own ignorance would have been disabling without generous cooperation of friendly experts. Explicit acknowledgment has been made in footnotes in most cases, but there are doubtless some regrettable omissions. Our sincere gratitude goes to all, named and unnamed, who have helped.

Contents

Reconceptions

in

Philosophy

and

Other Arts and Sciences

Abbreviations for books cited in the text:

by Nelson Goodman

SA *The Structure of Appearance*, third edition (1977), D. Reidel Publishing Co. (first published 1951)

FFF *Fact, Fiction, and Forecast*, fourth edition (1983), Harvard University Press (first published 1954)

LA *Languages of Art*, second edition, third printing (1976), Hackett Publishing Co. (first published 1968)

PP *Problems and Projects*, Hackett Publishing Co., 1972

WW *Ways of Worldmaking*, second printing (1981), Hackett Publishing Co. (first published 1978)

MM *Of Mind and Other Matters*, Harvard University Press, 1984

by Catherine Z. Elgin

RR *With Reference to Reference*, Hackett Publishing Co., 1983

PART ONE

▼

SURVEY

I

Knowing and Making

1. Obstacles to Knowing

The theory of knowledge to be sketched here rejects both absolutism and nihilism, both unique truth and the indistinguishability of truth from falsity. It stresses reconstruction over deconstruction, and tolerates neither the noumenal nor the merely possible nor any ready-made world.

Epistemology once sought certainty through derivation from incontrovertible basic statements. Whatever could be so derived, and nothing else, qualified as knowledge. Plainly this meant excluding much of what seems to have some claim to being considered knowledge. Since only sentences are subject to derivation, none of the insight, information, or understanding imparted by nonverbal symbols could count as knowledge. Maps, diagrams, pictures, and music could serve the process of knowledge only

Work on this chapter was supported by a grant from the University of North Carolina Research Council.

as auxiliary aids with no more than incidental epistemological interest. Moreover, by tradition, the only statements that constitute knowledge are those deductively or inductively derivable from literal basic sentences; so the understanding and insight gained from metaphorical statements or other figurative symbols is likewise excluded. And once the difficulty of deriving an 'ought' from an 'is' was recognized, evaluative statements went by the board as well. Ethical statements could not qualify as knowledge nor could methodological maxims, hypothetical imperatives, or rules of thumb, no matter how well they stood up in practice. That ascriptions of validity and soundness of inferences are evaluative was conveniently overlooked.

The justification for so narrowing the scope of epistemology came from the quest for certainty. Only within the indicated limits, it was believed, could certainty be achieved. The term "knowledge" was restricted to the claims that satisfy the highest epistemic or cognitive standards, and the field of epistemology confined to the study of such claims and the standards for judging them.

Since by now most of us are well aware that mistakes are always possible, the quest for certainty has been abandoned. No sentences are incontrovertible, and no modes of reasoning infallible. Even so, the traditional restrictions on the application of "knowledge" and on the scope and methods of epistemology have largely been retained. As a result, cognitively significant affinities between verbal and nonverbal symbols, between literal and metaphorical sentences, between descriptive and normative sentences have often been overlooked. Indeed, the exclusion of the evaluative, the figurative, and the nonverbal from epistemology has rendered their cognitive aspects all but invisible.

We want here to sketch an alternative epistemology that begins with release from these restrictions. Epistemology, as we conceive it, comprehends understanding or cognition in all of its modes—including perception, depiction, and emotion, as well as description. And it investigates the ways each of these informs and is informed by the others.

2. Structures of Experience

Empiricism maintains that knowledge depends on experience. This contention, although true enough, may be misleading. For it neglects to mention that the dependence goes both ways—that experience likewise depends on knowledge. Our expectations and beliefs about a situation affect the character of our experiences concerning it. They guide our investigations and structure our perceptual field. This is not to say that our expectations are always borne out or our beliefs always confirmed. Plainly they are not. But what attracts our attention is most often what defeats or fulfills a hope or a fear or violates a complacent assumption. What is routine often goes unnoticed. The insignificant typographical errors that leap to the proofreader's eye are seldom seen by readers concerned with the content of a text.

Beliefs and expectations supply systems of categories or kinds that structure what we perceive. And the structures they provide are various (*SA*, 127–149). A particular auditory event might be heard as a noise, as a piercing noise, as the sound of a trumpet, as a B-flat, as the first note of the fanfare, or in any of indefinitely many other ways. To characterize what is heard as the sound of a trumpet or as the first note of the fanfare requires a good deal of background knowledge. But every characterization relies on background knowledge of one sort or another. Even to recognize something as a sound requires knowing how to differentiate sounds from other sources of sensory stimulation, and how to segment auditory input into separate events.

Sensation is sometimes supposed to be primarily given. Doesn't a sound present a certain quality or set of qualities even to a person ignorant of its source or musical context? The trouble with saying this is that neither a sensation nor anything else comes already labeled. Our sensations, like everything else, are subject to a variety of characterizations. The range of available alternatives is a function of the conceptual systems we have constructed and mastered. If a particular characterization appears problematic, we can often retreat to one that is less so. Someone who wonders whether what he hears is properly characterized as "the first note of the fanfare" might unhesitatingly accept the characterization "trumpet B-flat". But the line of retreat is not foreordained. It depends on what is conceded and what is questioned in the context at hand. He might as easily doubt the appropriateness of the label "trumpet B-flat" while acknowledging that of "the first note of the fanfare". Indeed, he might accept both characterizations but be uncertain whether his experience is correctly labeled as "hearing" or "imagining" the sound. The descriptions and representations that can be invoked when others are disputed vary with differences in contextual features, including our interest in the situation, the background of agreement against which the dispute takes place, and the conceptual resources available to us. Together these guide us in choosing a characterization that is sufficiently uncontroversial to avoid begging the question, and sufficiently relevant to be informative and useful. But none of its characterizations is so basic, or neutral, or 'natural' as to be informative, useful, and uncontroversial in every context.

The ability to describe, represent, or recognize anything requires command of a system of categories in terms of which a domain is organized. Acquiring such a command involves learning what labels (verbal or nonverbal) belong to the system, what distinctions in the domain they mark, how such distinctions are to be recognized. Hearing a trumpet B-flat involves more than being within earshot when a particular noise is emitted. It involves having and exercising the ability to discriminate sounds on the basis of their source and on the basis of their pitch. Such abilities are normally acquired as we learn how to listen to music (*MM*, 146–150).

The mind then is actively engaged in perception just as it is in other modes of cognition. It imposes order on, as much as it discerns order in a domain. Moreover, things do not present themselves to us in any privileged vocabulary or system of categories. We have and use a variety of vocabularies and systems of categories that yield different ways in which things can be faithfully represented or described. Nothing about a domain favors one faithful characterization of its objects over others. To choose among them requires knowing how the several systems function.

3. Construction

In describing an object, we apply a label to it. Typically that label belongs to a family of alternatives that collectively sort the objects in a domain. Such a family of alternatives may be called a *scheme*, and the objects it sorts its *realm*. Thus "B-flat" belongs to a scheme that orders the realm of musical tones; and "elephant" to one that orders the realm of animals. A *system* is a scheme applied to a realm.

The alternatives of which a scheme consists need not be mutually exclusive. The scheme to which "elephant" belongs might include a label such as "pachyderm", which in its normal interpretation applies to everything "elephant" does, and to other animals as well.

Moreover, a scheme typically orders a realm in terms of implicit alternatives. In calling a tone B-flat, or an animal an elephant, we normally do not specify the interpretation of the remaining symbols in the system. Still, the range of alternatives to a particular classification can be important, for a single label may belong to several systems and be assigned different interpretations in each. According to a system that classifies in terms of primary colors exclusively, a particular bird is correctly said to be blue. According to a system that takes indigo and blue to be distinct, the bird must be labeled "indigo", not "blue". And according to one that takes indigo to be a shade of blue, both "indigo" and "blue" apply to the bird. Whether it is correct to call a bird blue then depends on the alternative color classifications that are admitted, even if the alternatives are not made explicit.

A scheme need not be exclusively associated with a single realm. A scheme whose labels include "tall" and "short" is applied to realms consisting of people, of buildings, of trees, and so on. And a scheme consisting of numerals is applied to any realm whose objects we care to count.

Likewise, a single realm is subject to alternative schematizations. A realm consisting of books, for example, might be organized according to the size, the subject matter, the intellectual merit, or the financial worth of its elements. Such schemes do not provide different labels for the same collections of objects; they sort the objects into different collections. Books alike in size differ markedly in subject, in intellectual merit, and in market value. To decide whether things are alike, then, we have to know what system is in play. A system integrates an expression into a network of labels that organizes, sorts, or classifies items in terms of the types of diversity to be recognized. It thus reflects or establishes likenesses; and systems that decide the matter differently may share a realm (*LA*, 71–74).

In speaking as though the objects in a realm are determined independently of any scheme that organizes them, we have been oversimplifying. For among the expressions whose interpretation is fixed by a system are "is identical to", "is the same thing as", and the like; and by fixing the interpretations of these expressions a system sets the conditions for the individuation of the objects in its realm (*WW*, 8).

Individuation is, as Quine says, determined by "a cluster of related grammatical particles and constructions: plural endings, pronouns, the 'is' of identity and its adaptations 'same' and 'other' ".[1] He neglects to mention that the interpretations of these

1. W. V. Quine, "Ontological Relativity", *Ontological Relativity and Other Essays* (New York: Columbia University Press, 1969), p. 32.

particles and constructions cannot be settled without considering the sort of thing they are individuating. They need to be interpreted as part of a broader system, and their interpretation varies as they are incorporated into different systems. Consider sunset. How we interpret identity, how we decide whether we are seeing the very same thing we saw yesterday, depends on whether we are concerned to identify suns or settings. The same sun sets day after day, but every dusk brings a new setting. What counts as being the same thing varies from one sort of object to another. It is the relation between Quine's cluster of particles and constructions and the other terms of the system that determines the conditions on the individuation of the objects in its realm. And under different interpretations, the realm consists of quite different elements.

Systems are not to be identified with languages. We have seen that terms of a single language may be incorporated into several systems and so participate in the sorting of different realms or in different sortings of the same realm. Moreover, not all systems are linguistic. Among familiar nonlinguistic systems are notational systems and representational (or pictorial) systems. If we look at the differences among these systems, the importance of certain syntactic and semantic features becomes evident.

One vivid difference between languages and pictorial systems is this: languages have alphabets; pictorial systems do not. As a result, linguistic signs that are spelled the same are recognized as syntactically equivalent. Pictorial elements, however similar, can never be syntactic equivalents. For without an alphabet, we have no way to distinguish between syntactically significant and insignificant differences among marks. There is no counterpart to spelling in pictorial systems. Languages are syntactically differentiated; pictorial or representational systems are syntactically dense.[2]

The important differences between languages and notations are

2. But see further Chapter VIII.

not syntactic but semantic. Many terms apply to each object. The sound of the trumpet might be described as "B-flat", "loud", "piercing", and in many other ways as well. But only one symbol of standard musical notation applies to the sound. Notations are thus semantically disjoint; languages and representational systems are not. Moreover, languages and representational systems admit of infinitely fine distinctions; notations do not. The trumpet sound might be called "loud", "very loud", "halfway between loud and very loud", and so on. But its characterization in terms of musical notation is unique; it admits of no further refinements. Semantic density is thus characteristic of representational systems; semantic differentiation is characteristic of notational systems.

Such syntactic and semantic differences are noteworthy, for they affect the order that different sorts of systems can produce. Representational systems, being syntactically and semantically dense, allow for infinite refinement at the cost of sacrificing determinateness. Just what symbols make up a picture, and just what items constitute its reference are never completely settled. Notational systems, being syntactically and semantically differentiated, guarantee duplicability. The exact syntactic character of any inscription and the unique class to which each of its objects belongs are determinable. Such determinability has its price: differences among compliants (*LA*, 144) of a single character are not captured by the notation.

Languages, like notational systems, are syntactically differentiated and disjoint. Thus the syntactic character of any linguistic token can be identified. This allows for repetition of utterances and replication of inscriptions. Like representational systems, languages are semantically dense and nondisjoint. Selecting a correct description may be difficult; for each object complies with indefinitely many terms. Moreover, we cannot always determine whether an object complies with a given term. The capacity for ever more refinement in the characterization of the domain makes it hard to determine whether any particular characterization is correct (*LA*, 130–154).

4. Constraints

Symbol systems are artefacts. Their syntactic and semantic features are not dictated by the domain, but result from decisions we make about how the domain is to be organized. And the systems we construct determine the similarities and differences we can recognize, the levels of precision we can produce, the degrees of determinateness we can achieve. Still, to say that symbol systems are contrivances is not to say that anything we take to be a system is an effective one, or that by mere stipulation we can make it so. And to say that alternative systems share a realm is not to say that the choice among them is arbitrary. Only after investigating the relevant standards will we be in a position to distinguish between genuine and spurious systems and to discover the features of our systems that make the use of different ones appropriate in different contexts.

Consistency is an obvious constraint on the adequacy of any system. No acceptable system can permit the joint application of mutually inconsistent labels to a single object. Consistency cannot be achieved by fiat; a system does not become consistent by our declaring it to be so. Indeed, constructing a consistent system of any complexity is hard work. Moreover, since the alternatives that constitute a scheme are typically implicit rather than explicit, it is often difficult to determine whether consistency has been achieved.

What then is the function of the consistency requirement? It tells us to employ only systems we think to be consistent. And it recommends that we scrutinize our systems for evidence of inconsistency. Such guidance, however, is secondary. The central normative function of the consistency requirement is to serve as a standard. It mandates that no inconsistent system is acceptable, that the use of an inconsistent system is an error. If at the time the system is used there is no reason to think it inconsistent, the error is understandable, and perhaps excusable; but it is still an error.

In system building we never start from scratch. Inevitably we begin with some conception of the objects in the domain and with some convictions about them. These guide our constructions. Our goal in constructing a verbal system is to organize a domain in a way that enables us to formulate increasingly many interesting and accurate statements about it. How can we tell whether we succeed? Since our presystematic judgments constitute our best guesses about the subject in question, they serve as touchstones against which to evaluate our constructions. For the most part, sentences previously accepted as true should turn out to be true when their expressions are interpreted according to our system; and sentences previously considered false should turn out to be false. The system should, moreover, settle the truth values of sentences which were previously in doubt (*FFF*, 66).

'For the most part' is crucial. If our antecedent judgments of truth and falsehood were decisive in every case, systematization could only organize and extend our claims to knowledge; it could not correct them. Systematization would be a means of preserving old errors, not an aid in discovering and correcting them. Instead, in the construction and application of a system, some previously accepted sentences may be given up and some previously rejected ones adopted in the interest of simplicity, uniformity, clarity, or consistency. But such modifications are piecemeal and programmatic. One foot stands firm while the other steps forward.

In addition to the more formal aims of constancy and consistency are considerations directed to the relevance and informativeness of our accounts. One important requirement is rightness of characterization relative to particular purpose (*WW*, 127–129).

Consider two systems of color classification: S_1 classifies objects in terms of our ordinary color predicates. S_2 classifies the same objects in terms of less familiar ones. Specifically, S_1 contains the terms "blue" and "green". S_2 contains the terms "grue" and "bleen" which are defined as follows:

x is grue $=_{df}$ x is examined before time t and is found to be green
or x is not examined before time t and is blue,

and

x is bleen $=_{df}$ x is examined before time t and is found to be blue
or x is not examined before time t and is green.

These definitions (and parallel ones for other color terms) ensure that the terms of S_2 are as clear and precise as those of S_1. If we can tell which objects are blue and which objects are green, we can tell which ones are grue and which ones are bleen. S_1 and S_2 differ only in the objects they take to be alike in color. Moreover S_2 is not in any absolute sense less fundamental than S_1. For the terms of S_2 and S_1 are interdefinable. If we take "blue" and "green" to be basic, "grue" and "bleen" are defined. But if we take "grue" and "bleen" to be basic, "blue" and "green" are defined. Thus,

x is blue $=_{df}$ x is examined before time t and is found to be bleen
or x is not examined before time t and is grue

and

x is green $=_{df}$ x is examined before time t and is found to be grue
or x is not examined before time t and is bleen.

We have here a clear case of two systems that impose different orders on a single realm. Which should we use? Plainly, the answer depends on what we are trying to do. Suppose we are engaged in inductive inference—in drawing general conclusions from limited evidence. If t is some time in the future, the problem is that any element of a contemporary evidence class that instantiates "green" also instantiates "grue". If all the emeralds examined to date have been found to be green, all of them are grue. Which hypothesis should we take them to support?

H_1: All emeralds are green

or

H_2: All emeralds are grue.

The answer seems obvious: H_1 is the preferable hypothesis. And clearly this preference generalizes. In projecting from known to unknown cases, "green" should be used rather than "grue". The difficulty is to say what makes it right to project "green" and wrong to project "grue".

Some seemingly plausible attempts to justify our preference are easily discredited. We cannot claim to base our current preference for "green" over "grue" on the knowledge that emeralds in the future will turn out to be green, not blue (and hence, not grue); for we have no way to know this. Nor can we maintain that "green" is epistemically more basic or more natural than "grue", for we have found no way to make sense of absolute epistemological priority. Since "blue" and "green" are interdefinable with "grue" and "bleen", the question of which pair is basic and which pair derived is entirely a question of which pair we start with.

5. Rightness of Categories

That question, though it may seem too accidental to have any function in the justification of our selection of categories, turns out to be surprisingly germane. Although "green" and "grue" accord equally with the evidence, we have long been accustomed to projecting "green", while projection of "grue" is nearly unprecedented.[3] Projection of "green" and familiar coordinate color predicates overrides introduction of novel color predicates like "grue". For "grue" cuts across our familiar categories and would require awkward revision of our practical and scientific vocabulary and our linguistic and cognitive practice.

Loyalty to entrenched predicates might be thought to result in petrification. But respect for entrenchment must not preclude use of new predicates. Rather it sets reasonable rules for their admission.

---

3. We project "green" when we apply it or any term coextensive with it to as yet unexamined instances on the basis of the instances we have already examined.

Some novel predicates do not compete with predicates that are firmly entrenched, but are adopted precisely because no entrenched predicate is satisfactory in a particular context. The term "quark", for example, was introduced to denote certain subatomic particles. Initially, of course, "quark" had no history of projection, and hence no earned entrenchment. Still, from the outset the term had some measure of entrenchment—entrenchment it inherited from related terms like "subatomic particle". These related terms had their own histories of successful projection. In introducing novel terms into a language that is used projectively, we often do so in ways that take advantage of the entrenchment of terms appropriately related to them.

Induction, of course, carries no guarantees. Even if its categories are projectible, an inductive inference may go from true premises to a false conclusion. Normally when this occurs, we blame it on inadequate evidence or bad luck. The discovery that, contrary to confident predictions, not all swans are white did not impugn the projectibility of the term "swan" or of the term "white".

Sometimes, however, inductions using certain categories regularly lead from true premises to false conclusions. Ultimately, such failures are reasons to think that the categories we have been using are wrong, and that others should be employed instead. Thus, for example, the history of failed Newtonian predictions set the stage for the replacement of classical physical categories by relativistic ones. The presumption in favor of entrenched predicates lasts only so long as their projection is inductively successful. Predicates whose projection leads regularly to false conclusions are unprojectible, regardless of their history. The bias in favor of entrenched categories thus does not preclude conceptual innovation. Novel categories may be fitted into a successful system or replace an unsuccessful one (*FFF*, 84–124).

Entrenchment is not, however, sufficient for rightness of categorization. The categories we employ must also serve the interests at hand. And different systems of categories serve different interests. To answer the questions biology sets for itself, for example, we require a system that classifies organisms on the basis of physiology. Thus whales are classified as mammals rather than as fish. Given the interests of biology, the physiological similarities of whales, camels, chipmunks, and raccoons is more significant than the differences in their natural habitats. In some conspicuous respects whales are very much like tuna. The issue of classification turns on the importance of these respects. Biology accords them little importance, and so assigns whales and tuna to different classes. When, however, our interests turn to saving, capturing, or killing the beasts, we need to know where to find them. The question of their natural habitat is then very much to the point. Accordingly we make use of a different system, one which cuts across taxonomic categories, classifying whales and tuna as aquatic, chipmunks and cobras as terrestrial.

Nor is rightness of categorization always a matter of entrenchment. In fantasy, for example, employment of unentrenched predicates is an effective literary device. Rightness in this case is a matter of providing a novel organization of a (real or fictive) realm—an organization that highlights hitherto unnoticed or often overlooked features and, perhaps, forces us to reconsider the appropriateness and adequacy of the categories we are accustomed to use.

Rightness of categorization can be achieved in other ways as well. In metaphor a familiar scheme is implicitly applied to a new realm or to its old realm in a new way. Typically, the result is a novel organization of the realm, for the metaphorical scheme classifies together objects in the realm that are not classified together by any literal scheme. Thus, for example, in calling someone a cactus, we apply a scheme that literally sorts plants to effect a sorting of people. If, as seems likely, the metaphor has no exact literal paraphrase, it captures a resemblance among people that no literal predicate does. Moreover, the metaphorical use of a term effects a likening of the objects in its literal and metaphorical extensions, enabling us to recognize affinities across realms (*RR*, 146–154). Once the metaphorical use of "cactus" is suggested, we have little difficulty identifying the people to whom it applies. Metaphor then enables us to avail ourselves of the organizational powers of a system while transcending the system's limitations. Established habits of thought guide the application of a scheme even when the realm it is applied to is new. Rightness of metaphorical categorization depends on factors such as these: whether the order achieved by the metaphorical application of a scheme is useful, enlightening, and informative; and whether the affinities it highlights between the metaphorical and literal referents of its terms are interesting, important, or otherwise apt (*LA*, 74–80; *MM*, 71–77).

Rightness of verbal categorization needs much more investigation, but I want first to examine rightness of nonverbal symbols. Since the symbols in question are not sentences, this cannot involve truth, predication, or induction. Still, pictorial, musical, and gestural symbols, and the systems to which they belong, are subject to standards of rightness—standards that are not all that different from standards appropriate to verbal systems.

Sometimes, as we saw, the relevant standards of rightness depend on what we want a system to do. A notational system, for example, is wanted in order to identify distinct items as instances of a single work. This requires that each semantic symbol of the system determine a unique extension, and each compliant determine a unique symbol. Then any two compliants of a single symbol will be instances of a single work. Severe syntactic and semantic constraints are required to achieve this result. The construction of a notation is subject to an additional constraint, for we don't want the class of performances that defines a work to be arbitrary. We have a practice of classifying elements of the realm as instances of a single work (for example, classifying diverse performances as instances of a single musical work). And an adequate notation should, for the most part, reflect that practice. Fidelity to our antecedent judgments regarding work identity is thus required of a notation adequate to define works. Antecedent judgments about work identity, moreover, limit the scope of such a notation. Since works in painting, sculpture, etching, and the like are not identified on syntactic or semantic grounds, no notation can be constructed to define them (*LA*, 127–130).

In painting, the term "realistic" is sometimes used to indicate a sort of representational rightness. A common account of such rightness is this: a painting is realistic to the extent that it captures the way its subject looks. Its rightness then is a matter of accuracy—of its being a faithful copy of its subject. The problem is that a given object looks many different ways depending on who is looking, from what point of view, under what conditions, in what frame of mind, and so on. And paintings that capture these different looks are not counted equally realistic. Moreover, many paintings that are considered realistic have fictional subjects. Their realism cannot consist in fidelity to what they depict, for they depict nothing. Realism seems to be a matter of familiarity rather than accuracy. Pictures in the accustomed, standard mode of representation are counted realistic; pictures in unfamiliar styles are not. If realism is a kind of rightness, the reason is that we have become so habituated to a certain representational style that the interpretation of works in that style is straightforward (*LA*, 36–39). Realism of representation, like projectibility of predicates, is then a matter of habituation.

There are other noteworthy parallels between realism and projectibility. Realism is no more static than projectibility. Novel ways of depicting may come to be recognized as realistic by being incorporated into, and so extending, the representational resources of the standard system. Moreover, a style considered realistic at one time may subsequently be considered unrealistic. Over time its representational resources are exhausted. It no longer portrays as plainly and unproblematically as it once did. The system is then superseded by another, and a new level of realism is said to be achieved (*MM*, 126–130).

Realistic representations, like projectible predicates, are right in contexts in which accord with common practice of one sort or another is desirable. Plainly such accord is not always wanted.

Like a description in terms of unentrenched predicates, a picture in an atypical representational system can be illuminating and rewarding. Unfamiliar symbol systems often provide new ways of presenting, ordering, or organizing a realm—ways that highlight features that the standard system obscures or ignores. The insight afforded then can compensate for the interpretive difficulty occasioned by the system's novelty. Such difficulty is, in any case, typically temporary. For we can learn to see and draw in terms of novel representational categories just as we can learn to comprehend and describe in terms of novel predicates. And as the system is mastered, difficulties in interpretation diminish.

In mastering a symbol system, we acquire the capacity to interpret particular works as symbols of the sytem and the capacity to interpret and reinterpret other things in terms of the categories the system provides. Thus, mastery of a cubist system involves not just knowing how to understand cubist works, but also how to apply the system's categories elsewhere—to resolve our visual experience into images consisting of lines and planes intersecting at odd angles and presenting several faces at once.

6. Symbol by Sample

Symbolizing is not always a matter of describing or depicting. Some items symbolize by referring to certain properties of their own. Such items are said to *exemplify* the properties they both possess and refer to.[4] For instance, a paint chip on a sample card exemplifies its own color and sheen. Paint that matches the chip need not be like it in every respect, but must be like it in color and sheen. Since the paint chip functions as a symbol, it requires interpretation. To identify the properties it exemplifies, we need to know the system it belongs to. The system for interpreting

---

4. In a strict nominalistic account of exemplification, talk of properties possessed is replaced by talk of labels instantiated. A symbol then exemplifies a label that it both instantiates and refers to. For this discussion such rigor is, perhaps, unnecessary.

paint samples is standardized and easily learned. Other exemplifying symbols are harder to interpret.

Exemplification is a central mode of symbolizing in the arts. A musical work might exemplify some of its harmonic, melodic, and rhythmic properties; a painting, some configurations of color, shape, and texture. To understand a work we need to know not just what properties it has, but which of them it exemplifies. And differences in the interpretation of a work often stem from disagreements about what properties are exemplified (*LA*, 52–67).

Exemplification is critical in the sciences as well. To construe something as evidence for or against a theory requires interpreting it as exemplifying properties pertinent to the truth or falsity of the theory. And to construe something as a valid or invalid argument requires interpreting it as a sequence of sentences exemplifying a logical form (*RR*, 87–90).

Inasmuch as symbols can exemplify only such properties as they possess, it might seem that the range of exemplification is relatively narrow. But this is not the case. Anything that serves as a sample functions as a symbol by exemplifying properties it is a sample of. Moreover, since an object can be described in indefinitely many ways, it has indefinitely many properties. In an appropriate context it might exemplify any of them. Finally, exemplification is not restricted to properties that are literally possessed. Symbols often exemplify metaphorically. Thus, a mathematical proof might metaphorically exemplify a property such as elegance, and a painting, a property such as poignancy. Understanding a symbol then frequently requires knowing what it exemplifies metaphorically as well as what it exemplifies literally.

Since different literal and metaphorical systems share a single realm, a symbol can exemplify a range of properties when interpreted as an element of the different systems it belongs to. A painting might metaphorically exemplify abject poverty when considered as a work of art, and future prosperity when considered as an investment.

Expression is a special case of metaphorical exemplification. Works are said to express only such properties as they metaphorically exemplify when interpreted as aesthetic symbols. The painting then expresses abject poverty but not future prosperity. Disagreements about what a work expresses are common. It is often difficult to say exactly what properties a work metaphorically possesses, which of these properties it exemplifies, and which of the metaphorically exemplified properties are relevant to interpretation of it as a work of art. By its cheapness of materials and workmanship, a building may exemplify the poverty of the people who produced it; but that is quite different from the expression of poverty in the design of a monument to a saint. The characterization of expression as a type of metaphorical exemplification does not by itself settle the interpretation of particular works (*LA*, 85–95).

To what standards of rightness are exemplificational symbols subject? Let us begin by considering fairness of sample. In sampling, our interest is, presumably, that the properties a sample exemplifies be actually shared by the stuff sampled. The pattern exemplified by a wallpaper swatch should be the same color, size, and configuration as the pattern on the wallpaper it represents. And the proportion of pollutants in a water sample should be the same as the proportion in the lake from which it was drawn. In some cases our standard of fairness of sample is accuracy— agreement in relevant properties of the sample and the stuff sampled. This is the criterion we use to decide if a wallpaper swatch is fair. In other cases, however, such a criterion is inapplicable. We study the chemical composition of our water sample to learn something about the lake. Rather than using our knowledge of the properties of the lake to decide whether our sample is fair, we use the sample to discover what the properties of the lake are. If the sample is fair, we can legitimately infer that the properties it exemplifies are shared by the rest of the water in the lake. But how do we decide whether it is fair? In cases like this, we consider a sample fair if it is fairly taken—if, that is, it is taken in a way that conforms to good practice in taking samples of that kind.

This, to be sure, does not guarantee that the sample is accurate. But in the absence of complete knowledge of the stuff we are sampling, nothing can do that. Our problem is a problem of projection—of deciding under what circumstances the properties exemplified by a sample can be projected onto a larger whole, or onto other samples of that whole. And just as agreement with inductive practice is required to determine which predicates are projectible, agreement with sampling practice is required to determine which samples are fair. Both practices evolve over time as we learn more about the domain under investigation.

Exemplification by works of art is like sampling from the sea. A work is right to the extent that the features it exemplifies can be projected to enhance our understanding of the work itself and of other aspects of our experience. Successful works transform perception and transfigure its objects by bringing us to recognize aspects, objects, and orders which we had previously underrated or overlooked (*WW*, 133–137).

Since symbols often exemplify several properties at once, a single symbol may be right in some respects and wrong in others. A badly cut fabric sample might rightly exemplify its texture and weave, even though its exemplification of pattern is misleading. A painting that rightly exemplifies properties of color and line might wrongly exemplify historical properties. So a painting that is a product of Edwardian England might not be a representative sample of works of that period. In that case it exemplifies properties that cannot be legitimately projected onto other Edwardian works.

That a symbol is a representative sample according to a system is not sufficient unless the system is appropriate. Otherwise the properties it exemplifies may be irrelevant. If, for example, we are concerned with the toxicity of our water sample, we need to know what chemical properties it exemplifies. That the sample exemplifies a peculiarly luminous shade of green is irrelevant unless its doing so is connected in some way with the range of chemical properties that concern us. If not, a system in which colors are exemplified is inappropriate in the context of our inquiry.

Rightness of exemplification then depends on a variety of factors. These include the properties a symbol exemplifies, the range of objects over which these properties are to be projected, and the appropriateness of the system to the ends for which it is being used.

7. Conflict and Multiplicity

Systems, as we have seen, are subject to multiple standards of rightness. In constructing a system, considerations such as accuracy, scope, entrenchment, and appropriateness are brought to bear. The difficulty is this: the standards of rightness we take our systems to be subject to and the goals we want them to realize may be jointly unsatisfiable. Then adjudication of competing claims is required to decide which combination is best on balance.

As we have seen, in constucting a descriptive system, we require that sentences antecedently deemed true be reflected as truths of the system. But this requirement has to admit of exceptions. For depending on what sentences we deem true, it can conflict with the requirement that a system countenance no inconsistencies. The conviction that vegetables contain no fat and the conviction that avocados contain fat cannot both be preserved in a system that classifies avocados as vegetables. As we systematize, the logical relations among sentences are made explicit. If inconsistencies emerge, the systems we construct must deviate from our antecedent convictions. A system might then interpret as falsehoods some of the sentences previously held true. Or it might construe as figurative some of the sentences previously taken literally. Or it might modify the boundaries of our original categories so that the conflict among our convictions dissolves.

In one way or another, our original judgments have to be modified to bring them into accord.

In other cases, the problem may be a tension between antecedently accepted sentences and our goals in systematizing. The classification of whales as fish would accord with our presystematic judgments about the domain. It would also complicate an elegant taxonomy designed to further rationally justifiable interests of biology. In biology the conviction that whales are fish is thus sacrificed to achieve simplicity of system.

The goals and interests we want a system to realize may conflict as well. If so, they must be modified, or some of them abandoned. In quantum mechanics, for example, we confront the incompatibility of the goal of a deterministic system with the goal of describing the realm in terms of its most basic constituents. Where we talk of individual protons and electrons, we must settle for statistical generalizations; where we speak deterministically, no mention of individual particles can be made.

In constructing a system, then, we seek to achieve an acceptable balance among competing claims. Both the character and the criteria for an acceptable resolution depend on a variety of factors including the range of presystematic sentences we expect our system to preserve, the goals we want it to realize, and the amenability of the domain (as we currently understand it) to the sort of system we seek to construct. Often alternative resolutions are equally reasonable.

Pluralism results. A number of independently acceptable systems can be constructed, none of which has a claim to epistemological primacy. In some cases different systems with a common realm answer to different interests. For instance, a system for constructing road maps is quite different from a system for constructing contour maps. The systems use different symbols, mark different boundaries, indicate different features of the terrain, and classify according to different geographical categories. A road map concentrates on man-made features—roads, bridges, towns; a contour map, on topographical features—hills, valleys, plains. A road map marks off political boundaries; a contour map, differences in elevation. A road map classifies as alike cities with roughly the same population; a contour map classifies as alike places at the same distance above (or below) sea level. Neither can be faulted for failing to provide the information that the other yields.

In other cases different systems balance off competing interests differently. One might sacrifice scope to achieve precision; another, forego precision to increase scope. One might trade cumbersome truths for serviceable approximations; another, exchange utility for truth. The choice among them depends heavily on what we want a system for.

Diverse systems may supply different resources for solving a common problem. In one mathematical system a problem might be solved algebraically; in another it might be solved trigonometrically. The solutions are equivalent. But they are formulated in different symbols and arrived at by different means. A criterion of equivalence of solution is not, however, always available. Still, solutions framed in several systems can be recognized as adequate. A perennial problem of representation is how to present more of a figure than is ordinarily perceptible from a single point of view. Different representational systems yield different solutions. In one the figure is shown directly and in reflection. In another, rather than a single figure, what is represented is a pair of figures which are, as it were, mirror images of each other. In yet another (say, a cubist system) the limits on what is perceptible from a single point of view are reconceived. Each of the systems yields an effective solution to the problem. And the availability of alternative solutions does not impugn the adequacy of any of them.

Our knowledge of a subject is enhanced as we come to understand the ways it is characterized by the various systems to which it belongs. In some sense, then, the several systems complement one another—yielding a deeper understanding of the subject than any single system alone provides. Typically, however, we cannot construct a single global system that comprehends the contributions of the several systems to our understanding of the subject (*WW*, 109–116). Conflicting, equally correct accounts of the motion of the sun and planets are obviously possible, and physics alternates between incompatible wave and particle theories. Again, the works of Jane Austen and those of Karl Marx contain telling descriptions of social conditions, and of the ways economic and social factors constrain our options and limit our lives. And both bring out the inequalities in benefits and burdens that follow from membership in different social classes. But the systems in which their accounts are cast employ different symbolic devices and make use of different categories. Austen's descriptions are fictional, ironic, specific, and expressive. Marx's are factual, literal, general, and descriptive. We cannot simply conjoin their accounts to arrive at a better understanding of social conditions, for we have no way to give a univocal interpretation to their conjunction.

A variety of symbol systems can thus be constructed which are neither reducible to nor justifiable in terms of a single preferred base. These systems, moreover, are subject to different standards, and there is no neutral standpoint from which all can be evaluated. But it does not follow that we can formulate standards in any way we please, or so construct a system that any claim we like turns out to be true (*WW*, 94–95; *MM*, 36–40). Considerations of consistency, fidelity to antecedent practice, satisfaction of our goals in systematizing, and adequacy for the purposes at hand admit of different specifications, receive different weightings, and are realized in different ways in the construction of different symbol systems. But none of them is achieved by fiat. The admission that there are many right systems and many standards of rightness thus does not collapse the distinction between right and wrong. If anything, it makes the investigation of that distinction more important.

Symbol systems are artefacts. Their construction and their application are subject to constraints. The interconnected questions of what constraints are legitimate, what symbol systems are constructible, what worlds they define, and what sorts of understanding they yield are central to epistemology.

(*Elgin*)

PART TWO

EXPLORATION

II

How Buildings Mean

1. Architectural Works

Arthur Schopenhauer ranked the several arts in a hierarchy, with literary and dramatic arts at the top, music soaring in a separate even higher heaven, and architecture sinking to the ground under the weight of beams and bricks and mortar.[1] The governing principle seems to be some measure of spirituality, with architecture ranking lowest by vice of being grossly material.

Nowadays such rankings are taken less seriously. Traditional ideologies and mythologies of the arts are undergoing deconstruction and disvaluation, making way for a neutral comparative study that can reveal a good deal not only about relations among

---

Laurie Olin and John Whiteman have given valuable help with the literature of architecture.

1. See Bryan Magee, *The Philosophy of Schopenhauer* (Oxford: Oxford University Press, 1983), pp. 176–178.

the several arts[2] but also about the kinships and contrasts between the arts, the sciences, and other ways that symbols of various kinds participate in the advancement of the understanding.

In comparing architecture with the other arts, what may first strike us, despite Schopenhauer, is a close affinity with music: architectural and musical works, unlike paintings or plays or novels, are seldom descriptive or representational. With some interesting exceptions, architectural works do not denote—that is, do not describe, recount, depict, or portray. They mean, if at all, in other ways.

On the other hand, an architectural work contrasts with other works of art in scale. A building or park or city[3] is not only bigger spatially and temporally than a musical performance or painting, it is bigger even than we are. We cannot take it all in from a single point of view; we must move around and within it to grasp the whole. Moreover, the architectural work is normally fixed in place. Unlike a painting that may be reframed or rehung or a concerto that may be heard in different halls, the architectural work is firmly set in a physical and cultural environment that alters slowly.

Finally, in architecture as in few other arts, a work usually has a practical function, such as protecting and facilitating certain activities, that is no less important than, and often dominates, its aesthetic function. The relationship between these two functions ranges from interdependence to mutual reinforcement to outright contention, and can be highly complex.

Before considering some consequences of and questions raised by these characteristics of architecture, perhaps we should ask what a work of architectural art is. Plainly, not all buildings are works of art, and what makes the difference is not merit. The

2. A recent contribution is *Das Laokoon-Projekt*, ed. Gunter Gebauer (Stuttgart: J. V. Metzler, 1984); see especially Gebauer's own essay, "Symbolstrukturen und die Grenzen der Kunst, Zu Lessings Kritik der Darstellungsfähigkeit künstlerischer Symbole", pp. 137–165.

3. Hereafter I shall ordinarily use "building" as the generic term for all such cases.

question "What is art?" must not be confused with the question "What is good art?" for most works of art are bad. Nor does being a work of art depend upon the maker's or anyone else's intentions but rather upon how the object in question functions. A building is a work of art only insofar as it signifies, means, refers, symbolizes in some way. That may seem less than obvious, for the sheer bulk of an architectural work and its daily dedication to a practical purpose often tend to obscure its symbolic function. Moreover, some formalist writers preach that pure art must be free of all symbolism, must exist and be looked upon solely in and for itself, and that any reference beyond it amounts virtually to pollution. But this contention, as we shall see, rests upon a cramped conception of reference.

Of course, not all symbolic functioning is aesthetic. A scientific treatise signifies abundantly but is not thereby a work of literary art; a painted sign giving directions is not thereby a work of pictorial art. And a building may mean in ways unrelated to being an architectural work—may become through association a symbol for sanctuary, or for a reign of terror, or for graft. Without attempting to characterize in general the features of symbolic function that distinguish works of art, we can proceed to look at some pertinent ways that architectural works as such symbolize.

2. Ways of Meaning

I am neither an architect nor a historian or critic of architecture. My undertaking here is not to evaluate works or to provide canons for evaluation or even to say what is meant by particular works of architecture, but rather to consider how such works may mean, how we determine what they mean, how they work, and why it matters.

The vocabulary of reference and related terms is vast: within a few brief passages from a couple of essays on architecture, we may read of buildings that allude, express, evoke, invoke, comment, quote; that are syntactical, literal, metaphorical, dialectical;

that are ambiguous or even contradictory! All these terms and many more, have to do in one way or another with reference and may help us to grasp what a building means. Here I want to outline some distinctions and interrelations among such terms (*MM*, 51–71; *RR*, 141–154). To begin with, the varieties of reference may be grouped under four headings: "denotation", "exemplification", "expression", and "mediated reference".

Denotation includes naming, predication, narration, description, exposition, and also portrayal and all pictorial representation—indeed, any labeling, any application of a symbol of any kind to an object, event, or other instance of it. "Berlin" and a certain postcard both denote Berlin, and so does "city", even though this word denotes other places as well. "Word" denotes many things, including itself.

Buildings are not texts or pictures and usually do not describe or depict. Yet representation does occur in salient ways in some architectural works, notably in Byzantine churches with mosaic-covered interiors and in Romanesque facades that consist almost entirely of sculpture (see Fig. 1). Perhaps even in such cases, we are inclined to say that prominent *parts* of the building represent rather than that the building itself or as a whole represents. As buildings that themselves depict, we may think first of shops that represent a peanut or an ice cream cone or a hot dog, but not all cases are so banal. Jørn Utzon's Opera House (1973) in Sydney is almost as literal a depiction of sailboats, though with a primary concern for form (see Fig. 2). In Arland Dirlam's First Baptist Church (1964) in Gloucester, Massachusetts, a traditional peaked roof is modified and accentuated to reflect the forms of sailboats as we approach from the east; and the frame of the nave, made of curved wood beams, is an inverted image of the skeletons of fishing boats often seen under construction in nearby Essex. Again, the weird towers of Antonio Gaudí's church of the Sagrada Família (Fig. 3), in Barcelona, are revealed as startling representations when we come upon the tapering conical mountains a few miles away at Montserrat.

Figure 1.   Saint Nicholas Church,
Civray, France, 12th Century

Figure 2.   Jørn Utzon,
Opera House, Sydney, 1973

Yet since few architectural works depict either as wholes or in part, directly or indirectly, architecture never had to undergo the trauma brought on by the advent of modern abstractionism in painting. In painting, where representation was customary, the absence of representation sometimes left a sense of deprivation and gave rise to both acrid accusations and defiant defenses of meaninglessness; but where representation is not expected, we readily focus upon other kinds of reference. These are no less important in painting or literature—indeed, their presence is a major feature distinguishing literary from nonliterary texts—but they are often somewhat obscured by our concern with what is depicted or described or recounted.

Whether or not a building represents anything, it may exemplify or express certain properties. Such reference runs, not as denotation does, from symbol to what it applies to as label, but in the opposite direction, from symbol to certain labels that apply to it or to properties possessed by it.[4] A commonplace case is a swatch of yellow plaid woolen serving as a sample. The swatch refers not to anything it pictures or describes or otherwise denotes but to its properties of being yellow, plaid, and woolen, or to the words "yellow", "plaid", and "woolen" that denote it. But it does not so exemplify all its properties nor all labels applying to it— not, for instance, its size or shape. The lady who ordered dress material 'exactly like the sample' did not want it in two-inch-square pieces with zigzag edges.

Exemplification is one of the major ways that architectural works mean. In formalist architecture it may take precedence over all other ways. According to William H. Jordy, the Dutch architect Gerrit Reitveld (see Fig. 4) "fragmented architecture into primal linear elements (columns, beams, and framing elements for openings) and planes (wall increments) in order to make visible the

---

4. I shall speak indifferently of properties or labels as being exemplified. For a discussion of this matter, see *LA*, pp. 54–57.

*Figure 3.   Antonio Gaudí,
Sagrada Familia Church,
Barcelona, 1882–1930*

*Figure 4.   Gerrit Reitveld, Schroder
House (model), Utrecht, 1924*

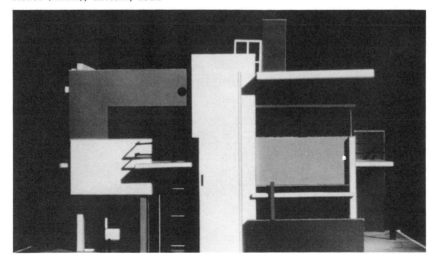

Figure 5.   Balthasar Neumann, Vierzehnheiligen Church, Bamberg, 1743–1772

'build' of the building".[5] That is, the building is designed to refer effectively to certain characteristics of its structure. In other buildings made of columns, beams, frames, and walls, the structure is not thus exemplified at all, serving only practical and perhaps also other symbolic functions. But exemplifications of structure may accompany, and either take precedence over or be subordinate to, other ways of meaning. For instance, reference to structure is not the primary symbolic function of a church but may play a notable supporting role. Of the Vierzehnheiligen pilgrim-

5. William H. Jordy, "Aedicular Modern: The Architecture of Michael Graves", *New Criterion* 2 (October 1983) 46.

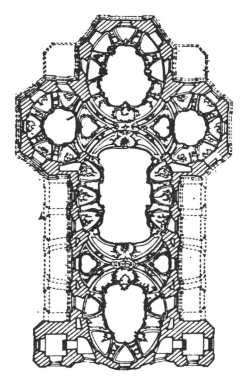

Figure 6.   Ground plan,
Vierzehnheiligen Church

age church near Bamberg (Figs. 5, 6), Christian Norberg-Schulz writes:

Analysis shows that two systems have been combined in the layout: a biaxial organism . . . and a conventional Latin cross. As the centre of the biaxial layout does not coincide with the crossing, an exceptionally strong syncopation results. Over the crossing, where traditionally the centre of the church ought to be, the vault is eaten away by the four adjacent baldachins. The space defined by the groundplan is thereby transposed relative to space defined by the vault and the resulting syncopated interpenetration implies a spatial integration more intimate than ever before in the history of architecture. This dynamic and ambiguous system of main spaces is surrounded by a secondary, outer zone, derived from the traditional aisles of the basilica.[6]

The shape of the church might have been correctly described in many alternative ways—the ground plan as a highly complex polygon, and so on. But, induced by the greater familiarity of oblongs and crosses and by the long preceding history of basilicas and cruciform churches, what comes forth, what is exemplified here, is the structure as derivative from these simpler forms. The vault likewise tells not as a single undulating shell but as a smooth shape interrupted by others. The syncopation and dynamism mentioned depend upon the interrelation not of formal properties that the building merely possesses but of properties it exemplifies.

Not all the properties (or labels) that a building refers to are among those it literally possesses (or that literally apply to it). The vault in the Vierzehnheiligen church is not literally eaten away; the spaces do not actually move; and their organization is not literally but rather metaphorically dynamic. Again, although literally a building blows no brass and beats no drums, some buildings are aptly described as 'jazzy'. A building may express feelings it does not feel, ideas it cannot think or state, activities it cannot perform. That the ascription of certain properties to a building in such cases is metaphorical does not amount merely to its being literally false, for metaphorical truth is as distinct from metaphorical falsity as is literal truth from literal falsity. A Gothic cathedral that soars and sings does not equally droop and grumble. Although both descriptions are literally false, the former but not the latter is metaphorically true.

Reference by a building to properties possessed either literally or metaphorically is exemplification, but exemplification of metaphorically possessed properties is what we more commonly call "expression". To mark the distinction, I ordinarily use "exemplification" as short for "literal exemplification" and reserve "expres-

6. Christian Norberg-Schulz, *Meaning in Western Architecture* (New York: Praeger, 1975), p. 311.

sion" for the metaphorical cases, although in much writing "expression" is used for cases of both sorts. For instance, we often read of a building's 'expressing' its function, but since a factory has the function of manufacturing, its exemplification of that function is of a property literally possessed. Only if the factory were to exemplify the function of, say, marketing, would it in my terminology be expressing that function. But distinguishing between exemplification and expression matters less than recognizing literal exemplification as an important variety of reference, especially in architecture. A purely formal building that neither depicts anything nor expresses any feelings or ideas is sometimes held not to function as a symbol at all. Actually, it exemplifies certain of its properties, and only so distinguishes itself from buildings that are not works of art at all.

I stress the role of exemplification, for it is often overlooked or even denied by writers who insist that the supreme virtue of a purely abstract painting or a purely formal architectural work lies in its freedom from all reference to anything else. But such a work is not an inert unmeaning object, nor does it refer solely (if at all) to itself. Like the swatch of cloth, it picks out, points to, *refers to* some of its properties but not others. And most of these exemplified properties are also properties of other things which are thus associated with, and may be indirectly referred to by, the work.

An architectural work may of course both literally exemplify some properties and express others. Of the facade of San Miniato al Monte outside Florence, Rudolph Arnheim writes that it "expresses its character as a self-contained object dependent on . . . the earth; but it also symbolizes the human mind's struggle for maintaining its own centered integrity against the interference by outer powers."[7] In my vocabulary the facade *exemplifies* the first (literal) property and *expresses* the second (metaphorical) one.

7. Rudolph Arnheim, "The Symbolism of Centric and Linear Composition", *Perspecta* 20 (1983) 142.

3. Ramifications

Representation, exemplification, and expression are elementary varieties of symbolization, but reference by a building to abstruse or complicated ideas sometimes runs along more devious paths, along homogeneous or heterogeneous chains of elementary referential links. For instance, if a church represents sailboats, and sailboats exemplify freedom from earth, and freedom from earth in turn exemplifies spirituality, then the church refers to spirituality via a three-link chain. Parts of a Michael Graves building may exemplify keystonelike and other forms depicted or exemplified by Egyptian or Greek architecture and, thus, indirectly refer to such buildings and in turn to properties these exemplify and express.[8] Such indirect or mediate reference is often termed "allusion", as when 'The Five' architects are described as making "allusions to ancient and Renaissance classicism" and as being "attracted by Le Corbusier's witty introduction of collage allusion into his buildings".[9] And when Robert Venturi writes of 'contradiction' in architecture, he is not supposing that a building can actually assert a self-contradictory sentence, but is speaking of exemplification by a building of forms that give rise when juxtaposed, because they are also severally exemplified in architecture of contrasting kinds (for example, classical and baroque), to expectations that contravene each other.[10] The 'contradiction' thus arises from indirect reference.

Not all chains consisting of referential links conduct reference from one end to the other. The name of the name of the rose is not the name of the rose; and "Gaudí's famous church in Bar-

8. Although a link in an ordinary chain is nondirectional, one element in a referential link may refer to but not be referred to by the other. Where one element exemplifies the other, however, reference runs in both directions, for the exemplified element denotes what exemplifies it.

9. Jordy, "Aedicular Modern", p. 45.

10. See Robert Venturi, *Complexity and Contradiction in Architecture* (Garden City, N.Y.: Doubleday, 1966).

celona" refers to a certain building, not to the mountains that that building refers to. On the other hand, a symbol that refers via a chain may also refer directly to the same thing; and sometimes where reference via a given chain becomes common, short-circuiting occurs. For instance, if a building alludes to Greek temples that in turn exemplify classical proportions that it does not itself possess, it may come to express these proportions directly. Moreover, reference by a work via a chain is seldom unique; a building may reach symbolically to the same referent along several routes. The reader will find his own examples.

Sometimes other relationships a building may stand in—for instance, to effects or causes of it—are mistaken for reference. What an architectural work means cannot in general be identified either with thoughts it inspires and feelings it arouses or with circumstances responsible for its existence or design. Although "evocation" is sometimes used almost interchangeably with "allusion" or "expression", it should be distinguished from them; for while some works allude to or express feelings they evoke, not all do. A building of an earlier era does not always express the nostalgia it evokes, nor does a skyscraper in a New England town always refer to the fury, however widespread and lasting, it may arouse. Equally, allusion and all other reference must be distinguished from causation. Even if in some cases "an epoch is inscribed in its monuments [so] architecture is not neutral[;] it expresses political, social, economic, and cultural 'finalities'"[11] still, an architectural work does not always refer to economic or social or psychological or other factors or ideas that brought about its construction or affected its design.

Even when a building does mean, that may have nothing to do with its architecture. A building of any design may come to stand for some of its causes or effects, or for some historical event that occurred in it or on its site, or for its designated use; any

11. François Mitterand, quoted in Julia Trilling, "Architecture as Politics", *Atlantic Monthly* (October 1983) 35.

abattoir may symbolize slaughter, and any mausoleum, death; and a costly county courthouse may symbolize extravagance. To mean in such a way is not thereby to function as an architectural work.

4. Architectural Judgment

So much for some of the ways that architectural works as such do mean and some they do not. But when does a work actually mean as such? Some writing about architecture may give the impression that prose is as prominent an ingredient in architecture as steel and stone and cement. Does a work mean just whatever anyone says it means, or is there a difference between right and wrong statements about how and what it means?

On one view, correct interpretation is unique; there are no alternatives, and rightness is tested by accord with the artist's intentions. Obviously, drastic adjustments in this are needed to accommodate works that fail to realize the artist's intentions or that exceed or diverge from them: not only the road to hell is paved with unfulfilled intentions, and great works are often full of unintended realizations. Moreover, we are seldom utterly at a loss to interpret a prehistoric or other work when virtually nothing is known of the artist or his intentions. But the main fault I find in this view lies in its absolutism rather than in the particular test of rightness specified. A work of art typically means in varied and contrasting and shifting ways and is open to many equally good and enlightening interpretations.

At the opposite extreme from such absolutism is a radical relativism that takes any interpretation to be as right or wrong as any other. Everything goes if anything does. All interpretations are extraneous to the work, and the critic's function is to strip them off. A work means whatever it may be said to mean—or, in other words, it does not mean at all. No difference between rightness and wrongness of interpretation is recognized. So stated, this view obviously involves a gross oversimplification. More than any other art, architecture makes us aware that interpretation cannot be so easily distinguished from the work. A painting can be presented all at once—though our perception of it involves synthesizing the results of scanning—but a building has to be put together from a heterogeneous assortment of visual and kinesthetic experiences: from views at different distances and angles, from walks through the interior, from climbing stairs and straining necks, from photographs, miniature models, sketches, plans, and from actual use. Such construction of the work as known is itself of the same sort as interpretation and will be affected by our ideas about the building and by what it and its parts mean or are coming to mean. The same altar may be a central pivot or an incidental deviation. A mosque will not have the same structure for a Muslim, a Christian, an atheist. Stripping off or ripping out *all* construals (that is, all interpretation and construction) does not leave a work cleansed of all encrustation but demolishes it (*MM*, 33–36).

The resolute deconstructionist will not flinch at this. He will dismiss unconstrued works as will-o-the-wisps and treat interpretation not as *of* anything but as mere storytelling. He is thus released from any stereotyped conception of a work and from the hampering and hopeless search for the single right interpretation. A heady freedom replaces oppressive obligation. But the freedom is bought at the price of inconsequence. Whatever may be said counts as a right interpretation of any work.

Thus both the absolutist's view that a work is and means what the architect intended and the extreme relativist's view that a work is and means whatever anyone happens to say have serious shortcomings. A third view that might be called constructive relativism takes deconstruction as a prelude to *re*construction and insists on recognition that among the many construals of a work some—even some that conflict with one another—are right while others are wrong. Consideration of what constitutes the difference thus becomes obligatory.

This question is formidable; for a work may be right or wrong in many different ways, and rightness reaches far beyond truth which pertains to verbal statements only. Obviously, no full and final answer to this question will be forthcoming. Not only is any search for a ready and conclusive test of rightness (for a key, no less, to all knowledge!) patently absurd, but even a pat and satisfying definition can hardly be expected. The particular determination of which works are right and which wrong is no more the philosopher's responsibility than is the determination of which statements are true in a particular science or of what are the facts of life. Those who are most concerned must apply and constantly develop their own procedures and sensibilities. The philosopher is no expert in all fields or, indeed, in any. His role is to study particular judgments made and general principles proposed on the basis of them and examine how tensions between particular judgments and general principles are resolved—sometimes by altering a principle, sometimes by changing a judgment. All I can offer here are some reflections on the *nature* of rightness and on factors affecting our tentative decisions concerning what versions are right or more nearly right than others (*WW*, 109–140).

Judgments of rightness of a building as a work of architecture (of how well it works as a work of art) are often in terms of some sort of good fit—fit of the parts together and of the whole to context and background. What constitutes such fit is not fixed but evolves. As illustrated in the case of 'contradiction' in architecture, drastic changes in standards of fit start from and are effected against some concepts and expectations that give way slowly. *Entrenchment* established by habit is centrally involved in the determination of rightness and is, indeed, the basis that makes innovation possible. In Venturi's words, "Order must exist before it can be broken".[12]

As an example of the judgment of rightness in terms of fit, consider Julia Trilling's discussion of Charles Garnier's Opéra in Paris (Fig. 7):

12. Venturi, *Complexity and Contradiction in Architecture*, p. 46.

Figure 7.   Charles Garnier, Opera House,
Avenue de l'Opéra, Paris, 1861–1874

Even Haussmann didn't always get the proportions right. The Garnier opera house, while indisputably monumental itself, doesn't really work to complete the Avenue de l'Opéra. It is too wide for its site, spilling over the sides of the frame defined by the buildings adjoining the avenue. In the case of the Place de la Bastille, the correct site for the new opera house would not be the designated one, on the old railway yards, but adjacent to it on the canal that completes Haussmann's Boulevard Richard-Lenoir.[13]

What is being discussed here is not physical fit; there is no complaint of blocked access or light or of intrusion into the public way. The fit in question is of exemplified forms to each other and into the form exemplified by the whole. It thus depends upon what the components and the whole signify in one way or another—in this case, primarily by exemplification. In other cases, fit may depend upon what is expressed or denoted or referred to via complex chains. And I am not suggesting that all rightness is a matter of fit.

13. Trilling, "Architecture as Politics", pp. 33–34.

To summarize briefly, I have tried to suggest some of the ways buildings may mean and ways that their meaning is involved in factors that affect judgment of their effective functioning as works of art. I have not tried to say how to determine what and how particular buildings mean, for we have no general rules for this any more than for determining what a text means or a drawing depicts; but I have tried to give some examples of the kinds of meaning involved. As for the further question, why it matters how and when a building means, I think that a work of architecture, or any other art, works as such to the extent that it enters into the way we see, feel, perceive, conceive, comprehend in general. A visit to an exhibition of paintings may transform our vision, and I have argued elsewhere that excellence of a work is a matter of enlightenment rather than of pleasure. A building, more than most works, alters our environments physically; but moreover, as a work of art it may through various avenues of meaning, inform and reorganize our entire experience. Like other works of art—and like scientific theories, too—it can give new insight, advance understanding, participate in our continual re-making of a world.

(Goodman)

III

Interpretation and Identity:

Can the Work Survive the World?

1. The World

Predictions concerning the end of the world have proven even less reliable than your broker's recommendations or your fondest hopes. Whether you await the end fearfully or eagerly, you may rest assured that it will never come—not because the world is everlasting but because it has already ended, if indeed it ever began. But we need not mourn, for the world is indeed well lost, and with it the stultifying stereotypes of absolutism: the absurd notions of science as the effort to discover a unique, prepackaged, but unfortunately, undiscoverable reality, and of truth as agreement with that inaccessible reality. All notions of pure givenness and unconditional necessity and of a single correct perspective and system of categories are lost as well.

If there is no such thing as the world, what are we living in?

We are indebted to Susan L. Feagin and Nelson Potter for helpful comments on an earlier draft of this chapter.

The answer might be "A world" or better, "Several worlds". For to deny that there is any such thing as *the* world is no more to deny that there are worlds than to deny that there is any such thing as *the* number between 2 and 7 is to deny that there are numbers between 2 and 7. The task of describing *the* world is as futile as the task of describing *the* number between 2 and 7.

The world is lost once we appreciate a curious feature of certain pairs of seemingly contradictory statements: if either is true, both are. Although "The earth is in motion" and "The earth is at rest" apparently contradict each other, both are true. But from a contradiction, every statement follows. So unless we are prepared to acknowledge the truth of every statement, the appearance of contradiction in cases like these must somehow be dispelled.

Why not just say that the conflicting statements belong to different accounts? According to one, the earth is in motion; according to another, it is at rest. This does not help. For according to a third, the earth is on the back of an elephant who in turn stands on a tortoise. The difference, of course, is that the last account is false; the first two, true. But then the contradiction reappears. In one true account, the earth is in motion. In another equally true account, the earth is at rest. Since both accounts are true, their conjunction is an account according to which the earth both is and is not in motion. And from this account, every statement follows.

Nor is the contradiction dissolved by simply relativizing conflicting statements to different frames of reference. For frames of reference are just coordinate systems within which spatial relations are mathematically represented. And admitting the truth of mutually contradictory mathematical representations is no less problematical than admitting the truth of mutually contradictory verbal ones.

The solution is this: conflicting statements, if true, are true in different worlds. A world in which the earth is in motion is not one in which the earth is at rest. Moreover, such worlds are heavily dependent on our accounts. A frame of reference or some

other representational system is mandatory for representing anything. And a variety of systems can be constructed. The mistake
comes in thinking of such systems as devices for representing an
antecedent reality. Rather, by determining the categories in terms
of which its realm is to be described, a representational system
determines the sorts of things its world consists of. Nor can we
factor out the contributions of the several systems and discover
the common features that underlie them. For to factor out everything version-dependent is to factor out everything. Although
there are indefinitely many true descriptions of the earth's motion,
there is no absolute motion that they all describe. No sense can
be made of motion (or anything else) except relative to one or
another frame of reference.

What is misguided then is not relativization to a system of
representation or frame of reference, but a simple-minded understanding of what such relativization achieves. If alternative
systems apply contradictory true descriptions to the same thing,
the difference between the systems does not mitigate the contradiction. But the situation can be understood differently. The apparent conflict between true descriptions shows that they are not
descriptions of the same thing. The earth that is truly described
as in motion is not the earth that is truly described as at rest.
And the world of the one has no room for a planet like the other.
So if both descriptions are true, they are true in different worlds.

There are then many worlds if any. Our talk of a world amounts
to talk of a true or right world version. And we make worlds by
making right versions. But notice the word "right". For philosophers like Rorty, Kuhn, and Feyerabend, loss of *the* world results
in a skepticism that despairs of distinguishing between what is
true and what is false, and reduces all science and other inquiry
to idle conversation.[1] For us, the rejection of untenable notions

---

1. Cf. Richard Rorty, *Philosophy and the Mirror of Nature* (Princeton: Princeton University Press, 1979); Thomas Kuhn, *The Structure of Scientific Revolutions* (Chicago:
University of Chicago Press, 1970); Paul Feyerabend, "Against Method: Outline of an

of a ready-made world and of truth as determined by it increases the importance of distinguishing between right and wrong versions. We can make versions at will, but making right versions (hence worlds), like making sofas and souffles, takes skill and care. For a version does not become right by our declaring it to be so.

Of course, with the world gone, rightness cannot be identified with correspondence to reality. How should rightness be construed? If we look to familiar kinds of rightness that are partly or wholly independent of truth, we find abundant clues. A deductive argument may be valid even if its conclusion is false; for from false premises a false conclusion can be validly deduced. An inductive argument may be valid even if its premises are true and its conclusion false; for inductive validity does not insure against improbable occurrences. A sample may be fair even if it does not accurately reflect what is sampled; for a fair sample is one that is fairly taken, and an unevenly distributed population may lack features exemplified by its fairly taken samples. Categories may be right or wrong even though, not being sentences, they are neither true nor false. Having been ordered to shoot anyone who moved, the guard shot all his prisoners, contending that they were all moving rapidly around the sun. Although true, his contention was plainly wrong, for it involved an inappropriate category of motion. A true sentence can thus be wrong through using inappropriate categories, and a false one partially right through using appropriate ones. From such observations we may try to develop a serviceable conception of rightness.

Systems of categories, sampling techniques, and argument forms are human contrivances. They are products of painstaking, continual, cognitive activity. And the various sorts of rightness to which our statements, samples, and other symbols are subject

Anarchistic Theory of Knowledge", in *Analyses of Theories and Methods in Physics and Psychology, Minnesota Studies in the Philosophy of Science* IV, ed. Michael Radner and Stephen Winokur (Minneapolis: University of Minnesota Press, 1970), pp. 17–130.

are dependent on the symbol systems we have managed to devise.

When we recognize that science does not passively inform upon but actively informs a world—that, indeed, a world is an artefact—we become acutely aware of significant but often overlooked affinities among art, science, perception, and the fashioning of our everyday worlds. The philosophies of these subjects are seen as aspects of a general theory of the understanding. We are moved then to undertake a comparative study of how various versions are made and how they function—to examine, for instance, the kinds of symbols and symbol systems and ways of referring involved (*RR*, 97–126).

The multiplicity of worlds, their dependence on symbol systems we construct, the variety of standards of rightness to which our constructions are subject—these are central theses of *Ways of Worldmaking* and *Of Mind and Other Matters*. We are not primarily concerned here to extend or defend these theses. We want instead to consider how such pluralism bears on the interpretation of literary works.

2. The Right Interpretation

The conclusion that there are many worlds if any is prompted by the discovery of separately adequate but irreconcilable descriptions and representations. The world succumbs to conflict among right versions. *Does the existence of individually adequate but irreconcilable interpretations of a text have the same effect?* Must we conclude that associated with a single text are many works if any? Does the unity of *Ulysses*, for example, succumb to conflict among right interpretations?

Pluralism about literature seems more plausible than pluralism about reality. The thesis that different interpretations define different works looks decidedly less dubious than the thesis that different versions define different worlds. So anyone persuaded of the latter seems unlikely to balk at the former. Alternatively, the conviction that a single text underlies different interpretations may seem, by analogy, to support the conclusion that a single world underlies different versions.[2] Still, there are important differences between the two cases that deserve to be investigated. They lead to the surprising conclusion that our grounds for pluralism about worlds do not extend to a like-minded pluralism about works. In one sense, of course, metaphysical pluralism guarantees literary pluralism. For literary works are denizens of worlds. So if there are many worlds in which *Ulysses* exists, *Ulysses* is automatically many different works. But this is not the problem that concerns us here. Our question is whether the availability of multiple right interpretations *of* a single text *in* a single world gives rise to multiple works associated with that text.

Controversy among literary theorists is rife over whether a work has many right interpretations or only one, over whether right interpretations can be distinguished from wrong ones, and—if there are many equally good interpretations—over what, if anything, constitutes the identity of the work.

However the work is identified, this much is clear: the various interpretations in question are interpretations of a single text. And that text can be identified syntactically, without appealing to any of the semantic or literary interpretations it bears. But there is no way to individuate a world except by means of a version; hence no way to identify a common subject to which conflicting versions refer (*WW*, 109–114; *MM*, 33–34). We can make sense of the claim that conflicting interpretations concern the same text, but not of the claim that conflicting versions concern the same world. But the question remains: Is a work to be identified with the text or with an interpretation of it? Is *Ulysses* its text or are there as many works as right interpretations of that text?

2. Cf. Alexander Nehamas, "Immanent and Transcendent Perspectivism in Nietzsche", *Nietzsche Studien* 11 (1983) 487–488.

The question need not bother us if there is only one right interpretation of any text; for then the work can be identified indifferently with the text or with the right interpretation—there is just the one text, the one right interpretation, the one work. That a text has a single right interpretation that is determined by and is entirely in accord with the author's intentions has been, and perhaps still is, like absolute realism, the most popular view. But like absolute realism, it is untenable. Even where an author's intentions are to some extent discoverable, they do not determine correctness of interpretation; for the significance of a work often diverges from, and may transcend or fall short of, what the author had in mind. Where information about the author's intentions is available, it may suggest interpretations of his work. But the importance of such information varies from one work to the next. For works do not always realize their authors' intentions. And even when they do, the realization of those intentions is not always central to the effectiveness or even the identity of a literary work. Understanding a work may be quite different from understanding what the author intended by it.

Whether or not the author's intention yields an interpretation, it certainly does not yield *the* interpretation of a text. For literary texts are susceptible to multiple interpretations. Multiplicity of meaning, subtle and complex ambiguity, is frequently a positive and vital feature of literary, as opposed to scientific, discourse. We disparage *Ulysses*, or even *Ozymandias*, if we suppose that it can be correctly construed in just one way.

Thus we are back to the question whether the work is to be identified with the text or with a right interpretation. If the latter, then *Ulysses* becomes many different works, with the interpreter at least as responsible for the work as the author is. The passionate pluralist and resolute relativist may welcome this, arguing that opposing interpretations can no more hold for the same work than opposing versions can hold for the same world, and that dissolution of the work into works is hardly shocking after the dissolution of the world into worlds.

But here there is cause for pause. First, the analogy between works and worlds neglects an important difference we have already noted: that while conflicting versions cannot describe the same world, conflicting interpretations may interpret the same text. The text, unlike the world, does not dissolve under opposing accounts. Moreover, no matter where the identity of a literary work is located, disagreement among interpretations differs significantly from disagreement among versions. Opposing interpretations concern a single text, whereas opposing versions have no common ground. Accordingly, nothing is gained by assigning conflicting interpretations to different works as we assign conflicting versions to different worlds. For the question how correct but conflicting interpretations can concern a single text is no less problematic than the question how they can concern a single work.

Second, if each right interpretation counts as a distinct work, what makes the difference between interpretations that in ordinary parlance are of the same work and interpretations that are of different works? Does an interpretation of *Ulysses* no more belong to the same work as another interpretation of *Ulysses* than to the same work as an interpretation of *Ozymandias*? That the first two are interpretations of the same text makes the difference.

Third, much of the rich multiplicity of meaning that is characteristic of many literary works seems to be not in any single interpretation, but in the very multiplicity of right interpretations, and this feature is not captured if each interpretation is taken to constitute a separate work. But can we perhaps consider the work to be the collection of all right interpretations of the text? In that case, works and texts will be one-to-one correlated, and the work can alternatively be identified with the text. Moreover, since the collection of right interpretations of a text may be countless and ever growing, we cannot identify the work by identifying the entire collection, but only by identifying the text. The text, unlike 'the world' (which vanishes behind our various versions), is at least as palpable and accessible as any interpretation. Diverse interpretations are grouped together by the text they interpret; and that text remains impervious to contentions among and changes in them.

3. The Text

But can the text actually bear the weight? What is a text? Are texts always readily distinguishable and identifiable? And is there always just one work for each text and one text for each work?

The question whether there may be more than one text for a single work is acutely raised by translations. If a translation from English into French preserves work-identity, then that work has more than one text. Obviously no translation retains all that is significant in the original. Even if the two are coextensive, reporting exactly the same events in as closely as possible the same way, they will differ somewhat in meaning. For their secondary extensions—the extensions of compounds of the texts and of parallel parts of them (*PP*, 221–230)—will not be the same. Moreover, they will inevitably differ, usually appreciably, in what they exemplify and express (*LA*, 45–89). Indeed, the translator of a poem typically has to decide the relative importance of preserving denotation (what the poem says), exemplification (what rhythmic, melodic, and other formal properties it shows forth), and expression (what feelings and other metaphorical properties it conveys).

In view of this, shall we consider even the best translations of a given work to be different works? Not too hastily, for we must bear in mind that right interpretations may differ as drastically as do good translations. We found reason to consider different interpretations to be interpretations *of* the same work, and we might regard good translations along with right interpretations as belonging to a collection that is determined by the work. What brings them together as being *of* the work is that they translate or interpret the original text. And the identity of the work rests on this text.

Interpretations and translations are themselves works. But they are not identical with the works they interpret or translate. Neither Harry Levin's critical study *The Question of Hamlet* nor August von Schlegel's German translation of the play is the work *Hamlet*. They are distinct works whose texts differ from the text of *Hamlet* and whose rightness depends on (among other things) the access they afford to the play, and the understanding they yield concerning it. Moreover, the texts that constitute Levin's and Schlegel's works are themselves subject to interpretation and translation.

But while there is only one text for each work, is there only one work for each text? To answer that we must first be clear about what constitutes *identity of text*. That identity is a matter pertaining solely to the syntax of a language—to the permissible configurations of letters, spaces, and punctuation marks—quite apart from what the text says or otherwise refers to.

Texts, of course, can be of any length, and for convenience we shall concentrate on very short examples. Take the word "cape". It refers ambiguously—sometimes to an article of clothing, sometimes to a body of land. But it normally does not refer to whatever is either such an article of clothing or such a body of land. Although ambiguous, "cape" is a single word. Inscriptions that refer to land masses are spelled the same as inscriptions that refer to outerwear. Moreover, they can be combined with exactly the same additional characters to yield syntactically significant strings. In the word "cape", then, we have a single short text. Its ambiguity renders it susceptible of two correct literal interpretations.

But now consider another equally brief example: "chat". This also has two alternative applications: to conversations and to cats. This duplicity may at first glance seem no more inimical to identity of text than is the ambiguity of "cape". But this case is different; for "chat" is not even the same word in French as in English. The difference in pronunciation is not a negligible feature; for a word has as instances or replicas not only written and printed inscriptions but also spoken utterances. And French utterances of "chat" are not syntactically interchangeable with English utterances of it. "Chat" in English and in French then does not consist of just the same group of replicas or instances, even though the classes of inscriptions coincide. What is more important, "chat" functions differently in the two language schemes. It differs, for example, in the combinations it enters to make compound terms and sentences: "chat" is an English word in "some chats", but a French word in "quelques chats". It is *a different word, a different text*, in the two languages. All this is purely a matter of syntax; the distinction is independent of what the words mean or refer to. It obtains even where, as with "permission", the two words have the same reference. And it obtains even where a single inscription functions in both languages at once. A note on the bulletin board saying "chat" might remind a forgetful Frenchman to feed the cat and a reticent Englishman to be more sociable.

A text is an inscription in a language. So its identity depends on the language to which it belongs. Usually the identificaiton of the language of a text is unproblematic. But not always. Some sequences of marks—"chat", for instance—occur in more than one language. Others occur in none. A configuration of marks might be a design or an inscription; and if an inscription, it might belong to any of several languages. We would do well then to consider the basis for identifying inscriptions and the languages they belong to.

The intention of the producer is not decisive on this matter. The indecipherable scribbles of a three-year-old are not linguistic tokens despite his intention to produce written words. An inscription of "chat" reminds Marie of her obligations as a cat owner, despite its having been penned to remind Maggie of her obligations as a hostess. And a bilingual's inscription of "permission" might be produced without any specific intention concerning the language in which it is to be understood.

Nor can the assignment of inscriptions to languages be strictly a matter of configuration, for the shapes and sizes of letters vary widely and independently of the languages in which their inscriptions occur. And as we have seen, the same configuration can occur in different languages.

Rather, marks are inscriptions in a language when they function as such. To accord a mark the status of an English inscription is then to treat it as having a certain syntactic role. Often there is only one language in which a configuration of marks can plausibly be thought to function. In some cases, as we have seen, there is more than one such language. In others, none. Since the text of *Hamlet* is unlikely to function in any other language as well as it does in English, its status as an exclusively English text seems secure. But "chat" functions equally well in English and in French, so its inscriptions might belong to either language. And since the child's scribble cannot be differentiated into permissible sequences of letters, spaces, and punctuation marks of any known language, it does not function linguistically. It is not a text. Nor is there any real problem about how inscriptions that are spelled the same, or how even the very same concrete inscription, can be two different works, two different texts. For almost anything may likewise function in various ways: the same chunk of bronze may be a sculpture, a doorstop, a weapon.

Thus a case like "chat" (and in principle there is no reason why a much longer string of marks might not constitute different texts in different languages) is not a case of two works having the same text but of two works with different texts. But are there, perhaps, other cases in which we have two works with but one text?

4. The Work

Identical twins, having lived closely together for many years, were sent for the summer to separate but similar camps in New England. Afterward each was asked to write a brief report of his experiences. Although the twins were reporting on distinct people, places, and events, their reports turned out to be exactly the same string of words. Is this a plain case of two works with the same text?

Unmistakably, we have only one text here. Unlike "chat", which functions as different texts in two different languages, this string of words is functioning in a single language. That the twins wrote down numerically distinct inscriptions and reported numerically distinct events in no way affects the identity of the text. The two inscriptions even if in different handwritings, are replicas of each other. They consist of exactly the same syntactic elements of English in exactly the same combination. And the identity of text between them is a purely syntactic relation. But where writers and subject matters are thus completely distinct, can there be only one work, or must there be two? If two, then identity of work does not always follow upon identity of text.

Here we are in danger of being misled by decorations. The remarkable twins and the improbable coincidence of text divert our attention so that we fail to notice that this case is basically the same as that of words like "cape". The common text has two different applications or interpretations. It does not matter that in the case of the twins the two applications are those of identifiable individuals who wrote down different inscriptions of the text, while the two different applications of "cape" are anonymous; nor does it matter that the twins case is unlikely to occur while the "cape" case happens often. In both cases, we have a single text with two interpretations. If we treat different interpretations as distinct works, we can take "cape" to be two words and the twins to have written two reports. But then we lose the distinction between a single work with multiple interpretations and a multiplicity of works—the distinction, roughly, between *Ulysses* and the many works of Agatha Christie. Since works with few right readings tend to be superficial, and works with many tend not to be, it seems unwise to sacrifice the basis for distinguishing between the two cases.

By now you will have recognized that the point of the twins example is much the same as that raised in a famous case devised by Borges.[3] Suppose, he says, that some centuries after Cervantes, a certain Pierre Menard writes a novel with the same text as *Don Quixote*. Menard's novel, however, tells a different story and is even, Borges says, in a different style from Cervantes', for in Menard's time the text is archaic whereas in Cervantes' time it was not. This case is widely taken to show conclusively that a work cannot be identical with a text—that Cervantes and Menard produced separate works with the same text. We contend, however, that the supposed two works are actually one. Menard can, perhaps, be credited with two achievements: having produced a replica of the text without copying it, and having formulated or inspired a new interpretation of the work—a way of reading it as a contemporary story in an archaic style with a different plot. But neither singly nor jointly do these amount to creating a new work.

What Menard wrote is simply another inscription of the text. Any of us can do the same, as can printing presses and photocopiers. Indeed, we are told, if infinitely many monkeys were to type for an infinitely long time, one would eventually produce a replica of the text. That replica, we maintain, would be as much an instance of the work *Don Quixote* as Cervantes' manuscript, Menard's manuscript, and each copy of the book that ever has been or will be printed (*LA*, 199–211; *RR*, 113–120). That the monkey may be supposed to have produced his copy randomly makes no difference. It is the same text, and is open to all the same interpretations, as the instances consciously inscribed by Cervantes, Menard, and the various anonymous copyists, printers, and typesetters who produced instances of the work. Questions of the intention or intelligence of the producer of a particular inscription are irrelevant to the identity of the work. Any inscription of the text, no matter who or what produced it, bears all the same interpretations as any other.

3. Jorge Luis Borges, "Pierre Menard, Author of the Quixote", *Labyrinths* (New York: New Directions, 1962), pp. 36–44.

Menard may in some way have proposed or inspired a new interpretation of the text. But no more than any other admissible interpretation offered before or since or by others does the Menard reading count as *the* work *Don Quixote*, or even as *a* work *Don Quixote*. All are merely interpretations of the work. Moreover, all and only right interpretations of Cervantes' text are right interpretations of Menard's. If it is incorrect for a contemporary reader to interpret Cervantes' text as archaic, it is equally incorrect to so interpret Menard's. For the 'two' texts are one. Just as we found that "cape", despite its two applications, is one word not two, so *Don Quixote*, despite its multiple admissible interpretations, is one work not many.

5. The Author

Who then is the author of a literary work? Since the work is the text, it seems reasonable to credit the individual who produced the first inscription of the text. Alternatively, we might take the author to be the individual who produced the first inscription that functioned as the text. Either way, Cervantes wins out over Menard by virtue of having produced the first inscription (or utterance) of *Don Quixote*. Both rules accord with our ordinary practice of attributing authorship. But they have implications that need to be acknowledged. The identity of a literary work is located in the text, and texts can be randomly produced. So the policy of attributing authorship to the first producer of a text might require recognizing a monkey or a machine as the author of a literary work. This seems absurd; for monkeys and machines cannot even understand literary works, much less create them. But the absurdity is only apparent. It is not unusual for a work to have correct interpretations that its author cannot understand. (Consider, for example, Freudian interpretations of *Hamlet*.) Works whose authors are monkeys or machines are simply limiting cases of this phenomenon. The authors of these works cannot understand any interpretations of them.[4]

Who is the author of the work the twins inscribed? If the inscriptions were produced simultaneously, neither twin has a greater claim to authorship than his brother. But they did not work together, so it would be wrong to consider them collaborators. The case is like that of simultaneous discovery in science, where investigators working independently arrive at the same result. In science, both are credited with the discovery. It seems best to do likewise in literature. Both twins then are authors of the report. We can distinguish between joint authorship and multiple authorship. A work is jointly authored if several authors collaborate to produce a single inscription of an original text. A work is multiply authored if several authors, working independently, produce separate inscriptions of a single original text. Multiply authored works are unusual, but they present no theoretical difficulty.

6. Beyond Literature

Our discussion has concerned literary works exclusively. Somewhat parallel considerations arise for works in the other arts. But what we have said cannot be automatically applied to them; for the locus of work-identity varies among the several arts. In painting, for example, each work has but a single instance. And the identity of the work depends on its having been produced by a

4. Although extreme, such limiting cases are not altogether fanciful. Computers are already credited with proving theorems when their input includes the axioms of a system and their output has the logical form of a valid deduction. At first, attempts were made to attribute the proofs to their programmers rather than to the machines. But these were conceded to have failed when it became evident that the programmers did not know how to prove the theorems in question and often did not even suspect that the formulas were theorems until the computers produced their proofs. If the inability to interpret their own results does not prevent computers from proving theorems, it is hard to see why that inability should be thought to preclude the production, by monkeys or machines, of other types of works.

particular artist and in particular circumstances. In etching, a work can have multiple instances, but their common history is crucial to the identity of each as an instance of that work. Although works of music and drama likewise admit of multiple instances— all the performances that comply with a particular score or script— in these arts, as in literature, work-identity is independent of history of production. Scores and scripts are defined syntactically; compliant performances are defined semantically. How a score or script came to be, and how a performance came to comply with it, are irrelevant to the identity of the work performed (*LA*, 112–123; *RR*, 113–120). Works of art whose identity depends on their history of production may be called *autographic*, works whose identity is settled syntactically or semantically, *allographic*.

The issue of authorship is, in a way, less important in allo- graphic arts than in autographic ones. For the very identity of a painting, etching, or sculpture turns on the question of who pro- duced it, and by what means. Nothing but a particular product of Botticelli's hand can satisfy the identity conditions of *La Pri- mavera*. The identity of a literary or musical work, however, does not depend on the answers to such questions. Who wrote *Don Quixote* or when simply does not matter to the identity of the work. In both autographic and allographic arts the identity of particular works is independent of work-attribution. Although the identity of an autographic work depends on its history, that identity is not affected by our knowledge or ignorance of its history. Of course, our understanding of any work is apt to be enhanced when we discover who created it, and under what circumstances. In every art we can expect to find works whose origins are unknown. And although the identity of the works is not affected by our ignorance of their origins, our understanding of them is likely to be.

Can the work survive the world? The answer these reflections seem to lead to is *yes*, but perhaps only under intensive care.

(*Goodman/Elgin*)

IV

Variations on Variation
—or Picasso back to Bach

1. When Is a Variation?

I want to explore here the notion of a variation in music, and
kindred notions in music and other arts. The music I shall focus
on is classical music in standard western notation. Such music is
a two-stage art: composition of a work results in a score, execution
in performances of the score. This art is also multiple: the musical
work consists of the several performances. And finally, such music is an allographic art: compliance with the score is the sole
requirement for a genuine instance of a work, no matter who
performs it; history of production does not affect genuineness of
an inscription or performance of the score.

A score does not prescribe performance completely or precisely.
Musical notation leaves some features unspecified, and specifies

I am grateful for the cooperation of Lyle Davidson, David Alpher, James Welu,
Konrad Oberhuber, and Jesús Mosterín, among others.

others only within certain tolerances. Thus genuine performances of a work may differ drastically even between those of equal quality. This troubles some composers, moving them to seek means of exercising greater control. On the other hand, some performers chafe at the constraints imposed by a score and want greater freedom for improvisation.

What must be stressed, however, is that the several performances of a work are *not* variations upon, but rather constitute, the work. However much they may differ, all genuine performances of a work comply with the same score, and no performance complies with more than one score. In contrast, a variation on a theme has a different score, and may be a variation on other themes.

A variation upon a work or theme or passage obviously must be like it in some respects and different from it in others. But that, after all, holds true for any two passages. What special musical relationships of likeness and difference must obtain between two passages for one of them to be a variation on the other? The Grove dictionary[1] begins by describing some elementary types of variation where the principal changing factor is pitch or harmony or rhythm, and then goes on to discuss combinations of and deviations from these along with all sorts of other cases. Some ways of making variations fall under such general ways of worldmaking as deletion, supplementation, deformation, reordering, and reweighting (WW, 7–17). Formulating an approximately adequate definition of the requisite musical relationship between variation and theme, covering even the commonest cases, is manifestly a complicated task. I happily leave it to the musicologist, and for now assume it done. My present concern is with subsequent questions.

Whatever relationship in terms of likenesses and differences may be required between a variation and a theme, that by itself

1. *The New Grove Dictionary of Music and Musicians*, ed. Stanley Sadie (London: Macmillan, 1980) 19, pp. 536–537.

is not enough; for the relationship of theme to variation is not symmetric, and furthermore, neither of two passages in entirely diverse works will function as a variation on the other unless they are somehow brought together.

In short, the question immediately facing us is "When is a variation?"; that is, "Under what circumstances does a passage *v* having the requisite musical relationship to a passage *t* function as a variation upon *t*?" This question takes priority over the question "What is a variation?" much as the question "When is art?" takes priority over the question "What is art?" (*WW*, 57–70). In both cases, characterization of a function precedes and provides means for demarcation of a class.

2. Reference in Variation

Our first try at an answer might be to say that if *v* has the requisite basic musical relation to *t* and is a passage that occurs later in a work beginning with *t*, then *v* functions as a variation on *t*. But that is both somewhat too narrow and somewhat too broad, and misses a central point. In the first place, the theme does not always precede the variations in a work, but may occur at the end or somewhere in the middle. Furthermore, if a passage *b* is musically related to another passage *a* in such a way as to make *b* eligible as a variation on *a*, then *a* is also musically related to *b* in such a way as to make *a* eligible as a variation on *b*. In *Variations on "America"* by Charles Ives, the theme appears at the end, reached by progressive extraction from the first, most elaborate, variation. In this case, the title and the familiarity of the song *America* unmistakably indicate which passage is the theme. Just how or whether one can determine without some such clues which among several passages is the theme is a question I leave to musicians. What concerns us here is the *significance* of the distinction when made. Plainly, that the requisite musical relationship obtains between two passages does not determine which is the theme, but is only a necessary, not a sufficient condition for functioning as a variation. What we have been missing so far is the recognition that a passage *v* functions as a variation on *t* only when *v* *refers to t* in a certain way. Functioning as a variation involves not only the requisite musical relationship but also a *referential* one. That calls for some explanation.

In what way, then, does a passage functioning as a variation on another refer to it? Not being a picture or a paragraph, a musical variation does not depict or describe the theme. And although variation and theme must possess certain common musical features, joint possession of such a feature by two passages does not constitute reference between them. An instance of a label does not solely on that account refer to another instance; two things may both be apples without either one referring to the other.

Reference by a variation to a theme is highly complex. In the first place, when functioning as a variation a passage does not merely possess but *exemplifies* the musical feature(s) it must have in common with the theme. To exemplify is to serve as a sample of a feature or label,[2] much in the way swatches of cloth in a tailor's or upholsterer's shop serve as samples of texture, color, pattern, and weight. Exemplification, as we have seen, *reverses* the direction of denotation, running back from instance to label, and is *selective:* a sample does not exemplify all its features—a swatch normally does not exemplify its size or shape—and an instance often does not serve as a sample at all. To exemplify is to bring out, call attention to, but not necessarily to stress a feature; a significant feature of the theme may be quite subtle,

2. No commitment to either nominalism or platonism is required by the present discussion. For those who, like the present writer, are nominalistically inclined, features are to be construed in terms of labels; and we may then speak indifferently of something possessing or being denoted by a feature. Those who are platonistically inclined will want to read "denoted by a feature" as short for "denoted by a label for a property". Either way, two points must be kept in mind: (1) by no means all labels are verbal, and (2) what is denoted by a label does not in all cases refer to that label, but in some cases (see below) does refer to it—by exemplification.

or somewhat hidden by changes made in a variation, so that exemplification emerges only after repeated listening.[3]

Referring to the musical features it must share with the theme is still not enough for a passage to function as a variation on a theme; the variation must refer to the theme *via that feature*. When the variation exemplifies the feature, which in turn denotes the theme, a route of reference from variation to theme is available. Still, that a passage refers to the feature and the feature to the theme, while providing two connected referential links constituting a path, does not imply that the passage refers along that path to the theme. When *a* refers to *b*, and *b* refers to *c*, *a* does not always refer to *c*. A name of a name of Helsinki refers to a word naming the city but seldom to the city. On the other hand, "The Cross", by naming a holy object that refers to Christianity, also refers to Christianity *via* that object. In short, referring is sometimes transitive, sometimes not.[4] When exemplification of the feature in question by a passage and denotation of the theme by the feature are taken as separate steps, the passage does not refer to the theme; but when the referring runs on through this two-link path, the passage refers to the theme via that feature.

Such reference, incidentally, is a special case of a type of reference that may well be called *allusion*: mediate or indirect reference along a path that reverses direction in a denotational hierarchy at least once (*MM*, 65–66). Reference from variation to theme goes in one direction (by exemplification) to certain common features and continues in the opposite direction (by denotation) from that feature to the theme.

Variation, though, plainly depends as much upon difference from as upon likeness to the theme. And just as functioning as

---

3. See *MM*, pp. 83–84 and the Monroe Beardsley article there cited.

4. See *WW*, pp. 41–56. But that discussion wants some elaboration to take care of further complications; for example, when a symbol *S* refers to *and contains* a symbol *Q* that refers to *x*, then whether or not *S* refers to *x* via *Q*, *S* may be said elliptically to refer to *x*—as short for saying that *S* contains something that refers to *x*. I leave such intricacies for another occasion.

a variation involves not merely having certain features in common with the theme but also referring to the theme via these features, so also such functioning involves not merely having certain features that contrast with the theme but also referring to the theme via such features. This raises a problem. *How can a variation refer to a theme via a feature not common to both?* How can a variation exemplify a feature it does not have? Or how can it refer to the theme by exemplifying features the theme does not have?

Consider for a moment how a giant can be called tiny. The term "tiny" is here applied metaphorically to something that not this term but a contrasting term applies to literally. "Tiny" denotes the giant not literally but figuratively and figurative denotation is no less genuine reference than is literal denotation. And figurative exemplification—that is, exemplification of a label that applies only figuratively—is no less genuine than is literal exemplification. Thus reference by a variation to a theme may be via a feature that literally belongs to one but only figuratively to the other. In this way metaphor is involved in *contrastive exemplification* and hence in variation.[5]

3. 'Formal' Requirements

In sum, we have found in our study two conditions on variation: a 'formal' condition and a functional one.[6] First, to be *eligible* as a variation, a passage must be like the theme in certain respects

5. Metaphor may be even more heavily involved where the contrasting features are already metaphorical, as when we have a sad variation on a happy theme. Here a further metaphorical step enters into contrastive exemplification. In effect, upon transfer from feelings to music, the scheme of labels is also reversed in its application to the variation so that the variation, by a double metaphor, contrastively exemplifies the happiness of the theme and refers to the theme via that feature. (Alternatively, the scheme is reversed in its application to the *theme*, and the variation refers to the theme via sadness.)

6. "Formal" or "musical" in the present context is not confined to what is in any narrow sense purely a matter of form, but is used for contrast with "functional" or "referential" as explained here.

and contrast with it in certain others. Second, to *function* as a variation, an eligible passage must literally exemplify the requisite shared, and metaphorically exemplify the requisite contrasting, features of the theme, and refer to it via these features. *Being* a variation derives from functioning as such: a variation is a passage that normally or primarily or usually so functions. A variation does not always so function any more than a work of art always functions as such, or a name always names, or a symbol always symbolizes.

I have examined the functional condition in some detail, but I gave the formal condition short shrift, promising to come back to the requisite musical relationship between variation and theme. Writers on music describe numerous types of variation and give the impression that new types are constantly being introduced. That makes formulating a general and projectible requirement a daunting task and raises the question whether, indeed, variation requires any musical relationship beyond likeness to the theme in any nontrivial musical respect and difference from it in any other. Does any passage referring to the theme via such features function as a variation? Can the formal conditions be dropped leaving only the referential one?

The answer, I think, is somewhat complicated. On the one hand, a formal requirement seems needed to distinguish variations from passages that do not count as variations at all but may refer to the theme in the same way. On the other hand, it seems clear that whatever formal condition is set forth, a musical relationship violating that condition may in practice come to serve as the basis for a new type of variation. Resolution of these contending considerations depends upon recognizing that while a formal condition is needed to exclude nonvariations that satisfy the referential condition, such a formal condition is only a codification of the musical relationship that in current practice distinguishes what are accepted as variations. Changes in that practice are not precluded. When particular judgments and general principles collide, an adjustment must be made by revising either or both (*FFF*, 63–64).

4. Improvisation and Parody

Among concepts closely related to variation, *improvisation* is presumably subject to somewhat looser formal restrictions than is variation. Otherwise, improvisation *upon*—that is, referring to—other music differs little from variation. A completely 'free' improvisation referring to no other music is simply a spontaneous invention having nothing to do with variation.

A *parody* of a work ordinarily meets the formal requirements for a variation. But while a variation is always upon a theme or work, a parody may be upon (or of) a style or a whole corpus of works; and the features exemplified and those contrastively exemplified are features common to works in the corpus. Of course the point of a parody is quite different from that of the usual variation. This may remind us that I have not so far discussed the *why* of variations—what they do, how they are used, what artistic roles they play. But I shall postpone that subject a little longer until after we have considered variation in arts other than music.

5. Variation in Various Arts

What I have said about music applies generally to dance. But important differences appear in arts such as printmaking that, though like music and dance in being two-stage and multiple, are unlike them in being not allographic but autographic. In etching, for example, the first stage consists in the making of a plate; the second stage, of printing impressions from that plate. Like the performance of a musical work, the several prints are the only instances of and constitute the work; and just as differences in players and playing among the performances may be great, so may differences in printer and printing—in ink, wiping, paper, and so on—among the impressions. *But* whereas in music genuine instances of a work are those performances, good or bad, that comply with the score, in etching there is no score, no notation. Genuine instances of a work are those impressions, good or bad, that are printed from the plate. Thus in etching—and other kinds of printmaking such as engraving, lithography, woodcut, and ordinary photography,[7] as well as in cast sculpture— history of production, not compliance with a score, distinguishes between what are and what are not instances of a work. Still, impressions are like performances in being instances of, not variations upon, the work. A variation upon a musical work complies with a different score; a variation upon an etching is printed from a different plate.

Painting lies at the furthest remove from music in being neither two-stage nor multiple nor allographic but one-stage and singular and autographic. The object produced by the painter is the work itself; there is no score or plate with multiple performances or impressions that must be distinguished from variations. But variations are distinguished from nonvariations on a work in much the same way in painting as in music and etching. A variation upon a painting is another work referring to it by exemplification of certain shared features and contrastive exemplification of certain differing features. Specifying the relevant features and spelling out the requisite relationship in detail may well be even harder than for music,[8] but the general principle is clear.

Painting and other pictorial arts differ from music, though, in some ways that bear on variation. One such difference is that in music, theme and variation are usually contained in a single work, while in painting the theme and variations are almost always separate works. Thus in music, variations are normally arrayed

7. But daguerrotype and some kinds of instant photography are, in contrast, one-stage, singular, and autographic.

8. Since some of the relevant features in music, though by no means all, can be specified in terms of the notation.

by the work in a unique linear order, while in painting no unique order is determined, and sets of variations without either theme or determinate linear ordering are not abnormal.[9]

Another relevant difference, that representation is much more common and more often important in painting than in music, calls for consideration of the relationship between variation and representation. We might suppose that a variation on a painting must always be a picture of it and also have the same subject matter. *Not so;* for example, a variation on a representational painting may be purely abstract, representing neither the painting nor its subject nor anything else. Conversely, a picture of a painting—for example, a picture showing the painting as seen from the back or the edge—is not always a variation on it. Even a picture that represents both the painting and its subject—for example, a slavish copy—need not be a variation on it. In sum, representation is neither a necessary nor a sufficient condition for variation. A variation must refer to the painting by way of exemplification of certain shared, and contrastive exemplification of certain unshared, features; and this relationship neither implies nor is implied by representation.

Yet of course a variation on a painting may also represent the painting or its subject or both. And paintings that are not usually variations on each other may function as such under certain circumstances. For instance, taken simply as pictures of Paris, paintings by several different artists do not refer to each other, and none is a variation on another, but when assembled in an exhibition, they may come to refer to each other in the way required for functioning as variations; and exemplification of the shared feature of representing Paris may participate in effecting such

9. Where there is no determinate sequence, variation is symmetric, but still not transitive. Although we may speak of a set of variations as 'variations on each other', that does not imply that every one is a variation on every other. It implies only that every one is connected by a path of variation-links to every other. That will be the case at one extreme where all the variation-links make up a single linear path, and at the other extreme where every variation is a variation on every other.

reference.[10] Likewise, a close copy normally functions as a picture of or a substitute for the original painting; but when the copy is juxtaposed and carefully compared with the original, certain differences may come to be contrastively exemplified, and the copy may function as a variation.

On the other hand, a copy that could hardly serve as a substitute for the original may be clearly a variation upon it. In a copy by an artist in his own style after a work by another artist in a very different style, contrastive exemplification may play a more prominent role. Rembrandt studied Leonardo da Vinci's fresco of the Last Supper (Fig. 8) intensively, probably from an engraving, and did at least three drawings, progressively diverging from the painting. The final drawing (Fig. 9), far from being a substitute for or memento of the Leonardo, is an *interpretation* of it in Rembrandt's terms—an exemplary variation. Benesch writes:

The drawing is the final result of Rembrandt's studies after Leonardo's *Last Supper*. Rembrandt has completely transformed the Italian composition into a work of his own creative spirit. The result . . . is a greater dramatic movement surging round the Saviour and rolling in waves through the composition. The pen strokes are split, confused, and vibrant with inner motion . . . by signing and dating it, he made it clear that it is to be considered an end in itself.[11]

6. The *Las Meninas* Variations

In painting, the most impressive variations are Picasso's studies of the Velázquez *Las Meninas*. Picasso first saw the picture (Prado Museum, Madrid) at the age of fourteen, and sketched it; at the age of seventy-six, some three hundred years after *Las Meninas* was finished (1656), he painted more than forty variations on it.

10. Since in this chapter the term "variation" is restricted to variations upon a work or part of a work, to speak of these paintings as variations upon Paris would be at best slightly elliptical.

11. Otto Benesch, *The Drawings of Rembrandt* (London: Phaidon, 1954) 2, p. 106.

The Velázquez shows the little royal princess in the center with a maid of honor on each side.[12] At our left is Velázquez, brush and palette in hand, before a canvas (shown from the back) that he has been working on. This work, a portrait of the king and queen, is partly reflected in the mirror at the back. At the right are two court dwarfs and the royal dog, behind them a duenna and a gentleman in waiting. At the rear is a palace steward holding open a door. The moment depicted is apparently just as the sitting has ended, with the royal couple about to pass through the studio and leave by the door held open for them; the dwarf at the right prods the dog to move out of the way.[13]

The painting was listed in early court inventories as "The Family Picture" but has come to be known by the name given to it in the catalogue of 1843: "Las Meninas", or "The Maids of Honor".[14] Why a painting with the princess as its central figure should come to be named for her attendants may be worth some reflection, and I shall return to this question later.

For those of us interested in reference, the painting offers an unusually complex network of six representational relationships: it represents the double portrait Velázquez is shown working on, and also a mirror in the background; the mirror represents (by reflection) the double portrait, and also the king and queen; and the double portrait and *Las Meninas* itself also represent the king and queen.[15] *Las Meninas* is unique and intriguing in many such special ways, discussed in countless papers. But Picasso is pri-

12. The Princess is Margarita Maria; the maid of honor at our left is Maria Agustina Sarmiento; the one at our right, Isabel de Velasco. The dwarfs are Maria Bárbola and Nicolasico Pertusato; the duenna, Marcela de Ulloa; the gentleman in waiting, probably Diego Ruiz de Azcona. The palace steward is José Nieto Velázquez. The name of the dog is not reported.

13. The interpretation in this last sentence, which I find entirely convincing, is due to Joel Snyder. See his "Las Meninas and the Mirror of the Prince", *Critical Inquiry* 11 (1985) 571, n. 27.

14. See José Gudiol, *Velázquez*, trans. Kenneth Lyons (New York: Viking, 1974), p. 388.

15. Note 6 above is relevant here.

marily concerned with something quite different. José Gudiol writes of Velázquez that figuratively "his ruling passion in life . . . perfectly realized in *The Maids of Honor* . . . is that of 'painting paint'".[16] Picasso shared this passion, and it accounts in large part for his intense and lifelong interest in this masterpiece of Spanish painting. That, together with his well-known fondness for children and pets, and the presence in his studio of a large reproduction of the Velázquez painting, must have prompted his choice of that picture as the theme for his variations. But along with his veneration was rebellion. Picasso's life was spent breaking away in all directions from the traditional ways of seeing and painting, and his set of variations is both a celebration of the Velázquez and also, as Lael Wertenbaker writes, "a summing up of the pictorial representations of form and space that Picasso himself had brought to modern art . . . a distillation of Picasso's life work".[17] What richer source of variations can there be than such a combination of concurrence and contention between visions?

Picasso's variations on *Las Meninas* are among the fifty-eight paintings he made and dated in the last four and one-half months of 1957. Forty-four of the fifty-eight are such variations, one (B.40) is a borderline case,[18] the rest are of other subjects (for example, in September he took a week off from *Las Meninas* to paint nine views through his studio window).

A prominent common feature running through this theme and variations is the depiction, in whole or part, of a constant subject

16. Gudiol, *Velázquez*, p. 291

17. Lael Wertenbaker et al., *The World of Picasso 1887–1973* (New York: Time-Life Books, 1967), p. 152.

18. The numbers preceded by "B" place the paintings among the fifty-eight in the order of production as given in the *Museo Picasso, Catalogo I* (Ayuntamiento de Barcelona, 1971). B.40 is not counted as a variation by the museum, apparently because, although it is based on the lower right corner of *Las Meninas*, it adds a piano not in that picture. I see no more reason for ruling this out than for ruling out musical variations that add to the theme.

matter. Another, more subtle, is the 'painting of paint' mentioned earlier. Among the variables are the selection of aspects and feelings of and toward the people depicted, along with features of drawing and design and style.

In the usual catalogue ordering, his set of variations is rather chaotic. The chronological order of production of the paintings cannot be taken as indicating a canonical order of the variations; a composer or other artist seldom works consecutively from the first to the final variation of a series but skips around as ideas occur to him. For the Picassos, where there is no need as in music to prescribe order of performance, there is not, except within certain short sequences, any indicated ordering at all. Nevertheless, the paintings have to be looked at in some order, and they relate to each other in interesting ways that suggest arranging them in various comprehensible and perhaps illuminating sequences.

As an example, nineteen of these variations are represented in the color plates[19] arranged according to subject: first, variations on the whole or a major part of the Velázquez composition; then successively, variations on each of the three major figures in it, taken from left to right. First, following the complete Velázquez *Las Meninas* are six Picasso variations (B.1, B.31, B.33, B.14, B.32, B.47) based on the whole or the central part of that picture. Next comes the left-hand maid of honor in the Velázquez followed by three Picasso variations (B.3, B.38, B.39) on this detail. Then the princess in the Velázquez followed by five variations (B.4, B.27, B.15, B.5, B.17). Finally the right-hand maid of honor in the Velázquez followed by five variations (B.46, B.51, B.53, B.52, B.58).

My selection and arrangement within each of the four groups is personal, but the guiding principles will be evident from the illustrations and accompanying comments. Like any other orga-

19. The original paintings vary in size from about ten by eight inches to about six and one-half by eight and one-half feet.

nization, this one involves interpretation, but with no claim that this is the only or the best interpretation or that it reflects any interests of Picasso's. Some notes on the illustrations follow.

1. *Velázquez*, Las Meninas.

2. This Picasso variation is also chronologically the earliest. Picasso was working, according to Sabartés, from a large black-and-white reproduction; and the present painting has little color. It is as if Picasso drained off Velázquez's color, preparatory to infusing his own. Two other aspects of this painting are especially notable. First, Picasso has let in the light, has opened the windows at the right so that daylight floods into the room; the light in Picasso's studio on the Mediterranean bursts in. Second, he has spread the composition out into a horizontal format. This suggests my reading from left to right. The figure of Velázquez here has become a kind of papier-maché hobgoblin, then appears very little in the other variations. The maid of honor at our right is viciously caricatured, but later (19–23) is shown in a very different guise. The royal mastiff has become Picasso's own pet dachshund, Lump.

3. The elements become more geometric, and bright twentieth-century color sharpens the complex composition.

4. The vertical format returns.

5. The design is simplified and almost circular, the space is deep and unified, the color more somber; the dog is black.

6. A flatter, angular, geometric pattern of hard-edged shapes in contrasting colors takes over. The dog is the livest element.

7. The three central figures are focused on here. The maids of honor dominate the diminished and devitalized princess. The mirror that reflects the king and queen in the Velázquez is here a blank square. Picasso was no royalist!

8. *Detail from* Las Meninas: *the left-hand maid of honor, Maria Agustina Sarmiento.*

9. The solicitous maid, painted with Van Gogh-like urgency, becomes an agitated, threatening figure.

10. The wildness gone, she performs a concentrated act of sorcery.

11. The sorceress reaches a paroxysm of witchery at the moment of taking possession.

12. *Detail from* Las Meninas: *Princess Margarita Maria.*

13. The princess, in near monochrome, receives the tray from the serving but grasping hands of the maid.

14. Clashing colors suggest internal turmoil.

15. The conflict and pain intensify in this compelling and penetrating portrait.

16. The color clashes have gone, leaving a stark record of torment.

17. Here the flesh is restored, the torment covered with courage, but the eyes and mouth poignantly reveal what lies underneath.

18. *Detail from* Las Meninas: *the right-hand maid of honor, Isabel de Velasco.*

19. The maid of honor begins a curtsey.

20-22. The curtsey develops into a dance.

23. In this final variation, which is also the final variation chronologically, the painting is richer, more detailed, and perhaps most Velázquez-like of all. The dancing figure contrasts sharply with the caricature of Isabel de Velasco in the first and some other variations.

7. Cross-Modal Variations

So far I have said nothing about cross-modal variations. Some features, such as feelings and aspects of design and style are common to painting and music; and a work in one medium may refer to a work in another via such features. What might musical variations paralleling Picasso's painted variations on *Las Meninas* be like? Composer David Alpher was enough intrigued with this question to spend some months composing a theme and twenty-two variations—for piano, oboe, guitar, and cello—correlated with the Velázquez and a selection of the Picassos in an arrangement I suggested.[20]

Earlier in this paper I postponed the question of the *why* of variation—of what is accomplished cognitively and aesthetically by variation. The best answer, I think, can come from looking at such examples as the Picasso variations, listening to the music in conjunction with such looking, and observing the effect of such experiences. Variations upon a work, whether in the same or a different medium—and still more, sets of variations—are interpretations of the work; the Picasso variations function as much in this way as does an illuminating essay on *Las Meninas*. Like all other interpretations in paint or music or words, variations are works in their own right, though they may enhance and be enhanced by the theme. Variations and theme reflect each other; *Las Meninas* and the Picassos alike lose when either is deprived of the others. And incidentally, the Picassos, painted more than one hundred years after *The Family Portrait* became *The Maids of Honor*, vividly explain that change, showing the maids of honor as the psychologically dominant persons in the scene.

(*Goodman*)

20. Alpher composed the *Las Meninas Variation* in 1985 for a program called *Variations* based on a lecture along the lines of the present chapter, the slides, and the music. The program in various forms has been presented at the University of Helsinki, Wayne State University, the Rockport (Massachusetts) Chamber Music Festival, Harvard University, and Trinity University (Texas).

Figure 8   Leonardo da Vinci, *The Last Supper*, Sta. Maria del Grazie,
            Milan, 1495–1498

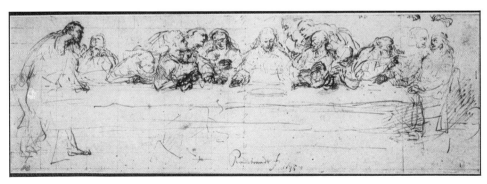

Figure 9   Rembrandt van Rijn, *The Last Supper* (after Leonardo da Vinci),
            Kupperstichkabinett, Berlin, 1635.

1

2

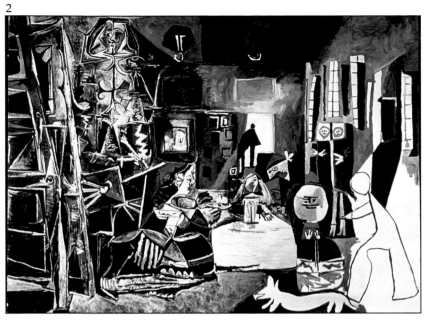

3

4

5

6

7

12

13

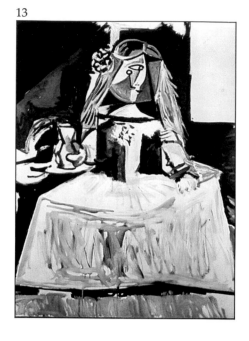

14

15

16

17

18

19

20

21

22

23

V

Sights Unseen

1. Dilemma

In characterizing cognitive psychology, Howard Gardner writes, "in talking about human cognitive activities, it is necessary to speak about mental representations".[1] The literature of cognitive psychology offers an abundance of such fascinating talk, including circumstantial reports of encounters with and experiments upon mental imagery. Yet cognitive psychology has been engaged from its beginnings in a life-and-death struggle over the very existence of pictures in the mind. Sometimes a psychologist's most assiduous accounts of phenomena of mental imagery have the flavor of tracts by impassioned believers in flying saucers. And the

---

1. *The Mind's New Science* (New York: Basic Books, 1985), p. 6. Two chapters of this book are especially relevant to our present discussion: chapter 1, on the distinguishing features of cognitive psychology, and chapter 11, on the question whether mental images are themselves mere 'figments of the imagination'.

flames of controversy feed on the stubborn resistance of behaviorists, physicalists, and acidulous philosophers.

In the present discussion, the term "mental images" applies to images of memory and imagination as distinguished both from material images such as paintings and from optical and other sensory images. However, I shall often shorten "mental image" to "image", taking "mental" as understood. Mental images, although they include 'pictures in the mind', are not all pictorial; some, for example, are musical and some are verbal.[2]

On the one hand, we talk quite confidently of the mental images we have, of their clarity or vagueness, of details present or missing, of manipulating and experimenting on such images. We can describe them, picture them, compare them with other images or with their objects. We know what it is to succeed or fail in trying to conjure up an image, and can compare our own experience of images with that of other people. Indeed, discourse about images is in this sense hardly less intersubjective than discourse about objects. And our talk of images, so central to cognitive psychology, seems surely not to consist of fairy tales but to be serious, significant, and at its best scientific. That we have images and can report on them with reasonable reliability is incontestable, isn't it?

And yet—and yet—on the other hand, what *are* these pictures in the mind? They are pictures not painted, drawn, engraved, photographed—not in any material medium. And they are invisible, intangible, altogether insensible. A visual image cannot be seen (for seeing requires looking at something before the eyes); an auditory image makes no noise; and the pain in my toe I can now imagine does not hurt. Again, whatever mental images may be, where are they? There is no small theater in the head where these images are projected on a screen, and there is nobody there to look at them anyway. When we are asked what or where

2. On verbal images see further *MM*, pp. 21–28. The present chapter is a sequel to that discussion, titled "On Thoughts without Words".

mental images are, we falter. Our answers are negative and self-defeating. When the mental image goes on trial, testimony for the defense is itself enough for conviction. The mental image seems to be unimaginable, a mere figment of the imagination! Or, in words less minced, the inevitable conclusion seems to be that there are no mental images.

How shall we resolve this dilemma? Shall we, deciding that the talk of mental imagery in everyday life and cognitive psychology is indispensable and veridical, simply suffer in silence the embarrassing questions asked by philosophers and other troublemakers? Or shall we, deciding that no one in his right mind could ever find any pictures there, just dismiss all talk of mental images as so much vacuous verbiage? I think we are stuck with both horns of the dilemma: that we can talk significantly about mental images but that there are none.

2. Psychology and Mythology

Having painted myself into that corner, I may do well to change the subject. Let's talk of centaurs or of Don Quixote. A centaur has a man's head and torso and a horse's rear; has four legs, not two or six, and no horns. Don Quixote wears a beard, and is Spanish not Greek. He is heroically and pathetically and delightfully daft, rides a horse named Rosinante, and has a servant named Sancho Panza. We can distinguish centaurs from unicorns and mermaids, and Don Quixote from Winston Churchill and Rip van Winkle. In short, we know a good deal about centaurs and about Don Quixote. And yet, and yet, there are no centaurs, there is no Don Quixote.

How then can I know about them? To begin with, while there are no centaurs, there are descriptions, stories, pictures of them.[3] And we know something about centaurs to the extent that we

---

3. The ensuing discussion applies an idea explained and developed in my papers "On Likeness of Meaning" (1949) and "On Some Differences about Meaning" (1953). Both are reprinted in *PP*, pp. 221–238.

can judge or produce descriptions or pictures of centaurs, sort out descriptions and pictures that are of centaurs from those that are not, accept right ones and reject or criticize or revise wrong ones. But isn't this begging the question? For if there are no centaurs, how can there be pictures *of* them? Our language misleads us here. A picture said to be of a centaur, or a description said to be of Don Quixote, does not actually depict or describe anything, since there is nothing for it to describe or depict. Rather, it is a picture or description belonging to a certain kind; and to block seductive wrong inferences, we may do better to call it a centaur picture or Don Quixote description. We classify fictive pictures and descriptions not through having examined anything they depict or describe but—just as we classify furniture into chairs, tables, desks, and so on—through having learned the application of the predicates in question.

What we say ostensibly about centaurs or Don Quixote thus has to be interpreted in terms of discourse about centaur (or Don Quixote) pictures or descriptions. When we say that centaurs differ from unicorns and from Don Quixote we don't mean to be taken at our word; for strictly, since none of these exists, all centaurs are unicorns, all unicorns are centaurs, and Don Quixote is both unicorn and centaur. To know that centaurs differ from unicorns and from Don Quixote is to know that centaur pictures and descriptions differ from unicorn pictures and descriptions and from Don Quixote pictures and descriptions. What we ordinarily call knowledge about centaurs or Don Quixote is, speaking more carefully, centaur knowledge or Don Quixote knowledge.

By now, of course, the point of my fabulous digression has been obvious for some time. If we can talk sensibly and responsibly about (that is, ostensibly about) centaurs although there are none and Don Quixote who never was, can we perhaps talk likewise about mental images although there are none?[4] Can I

4. After writing this chapter, I found that a central thesis—the assimilation of image talk to fiction—and some other points were included in two of Daniel Dennett's

say that there are no mental images and yet say quite intelligibly and truly that I now have in my mind a picture of Capri? Yes, if having that image is construed in terms of my ability to describe or picture or sort out descriptions or pictures of the image— though any descriptions or pictures I produce or encounter will not be *of* the image but rather be image descriptions and image pictures.

If here we seem headed toward absorbing cognitive psychology into mythology or fiction, that may be an unwelcome prospect for some, though hardly inappropriate when conferences on the subject have come to include novelists and opera directors along with psychologists.[5] But let's postpone bemoaning or rejoicing until we have looked a little more closely into what is involved.

Notice first that in likening psychology to fiction, I am no more denying the genuineness of images than I am denying the genuineness of centaur knowledge or Don Quixote knowledge. Centaur descriptions or Don Quixote pictures may be right or wrong. In checking on them we go back to classical literature and iconography[6] or to the works of Cervantes and his commentators and illustrators, and so on. In checking on talk of images, we have no Greek fables or Spanish tales, but something more like a continuing soap opera or several of them—a growing corpus of our own and others' verbal and pictorial discourse and the reports of psychologists. Thus in all these cases there are standards of rightness—not comprehensive, absolute, fixed standards, but standards with some stability. And that, indeed, is all we have for discourse about absent acutal objects (*WW*, 109–140).

---

writings: *Brainstorms* (Cambridge, Mass: MIT Press, 1978), chapter 10, "Two Approaches to Mental Images", pp. 174–180; and "How to Study Human Consciousness Empirically, or Nothing Comes to Mind", *Synthese* 53 (1982) 159–180. My own development of these ideas grew out of my earlier work on likeness of meaning, fictive representation, and 'thoughts without words', and is integrally related to my whole treatment of the ways fictional and other symbols function.

5. This refers to the conference "Images and Understanding", held in London in 1986, which included an earlier version of the present chapter.

6. And later writers such as John Updike!

Even for present objects, usually a rather small part of what we know results from direct examination. Questions about Don Quixote's life are as open to investigation as questions about Napoleon's; and whether proposed answers are right or wrong can be legitimately debated in both cases. Psychology and mythology are related in much the same way, and neither need feel demeaned by its affinity with the other.

3. Images and Action

Translation of talk about nothing into talk about something often takes some trouble. I said a moment ago that centaurs differ from unicorns in that centaur pictures and descriptions differ from unicorn pictures and descriptions. To "centaur pictures and descriptions and unicorn pictures and descriptions" we may well add "and centaur images and unicorn images" since centaur images and unicorn images also differ. But then we must remember that since there are no such images (or any other images), talk ostensibly about them must be treated in the same way as talk of centaurs and unicorns, so the expanded statement will read: Centaurs differ from unicorns in that centaur pictures and descriptions differ from unicorn pictures and descriptions, and in that centaur-image pictures and descriptions differ from unicorn-image pictures and descriptions.

This brings up the question how an image picture, say a certain centaur-image picture or a horse-image picture, can be told from a centaur picture or a horse picture. A blurry horse picture is surely not a picture of a blurry horse; the blurriness belongs to the picture or the image. But is the picture before us a blurry picture of a horse, or a blurry picture of a horse-image or a picture of a blurry horse-image? That is, is it a blurry horse picture or a blurry horse-image picture or a blurry-horse-image picture? Sometimes that will be doubtful, and we may have to look to descriptions, to verbal reports and answers to questions. But these cannot always be taken at face value. A request to describe a given image as such is easily confused with a request to say what it is an image of. Furthermore, we seldom take due account of such oddities of depiction as that a picture of a horse-picture is not always a horse picture, that a picture of a picture need not be a copy of it, that some (abstract) pictures are not even fictively pictures of anything, and that a picture of a picture of nothing is still a picture of something. Such complications are not peculiar to our present discussion but arise in the underlying general theory of representation. I mention them here only to illustrate how the tightening of loose talk about images can call for a good deal of care.

In view of all this, what is to be done? Perhaps, weary of such sophistry, we may be inclined simply to jettison all talk of nothing as worth nothing, to condemn as nonsense all talk ostensibly about mental images. But that would be to condemn an indispensable part of ordinary and psychological discourse on grounds such as would serve, no less plausibly, for condemning the works of Cervantes and Shakespeare.

In contrast, the cognitive psychologist may be glad to hear that there is a way of making sense of talk about mental images, and take comfort in the thought that the availability of an automatic process for purifying talk of images leaves him free to go on exactly as before, and refer all queries to the philosopher. But the treatment of image talk I have been suggesting is not a quick and easy excision of some pseudoentities; it does not amount to translation by routine application of a simple formula. Indeed, although I have spoken loosely of it as translation, it is hardly that; for translation of nonsense would presumably still be nonsense. Rather, what goes on is replacement of statements ostensibly about images by statements about objects and events. That cannot complacently be left until after the psychological investigations have been carried out in ordinary parlance; for our image talk raw and unprocessed is a terrible tangle. To accept at face value both the statement that there are no mental images and the statement that I have one in my mind is to forgo all consistency. If we give up the former statement and say that there *are* mental images, we face innumerable unanswerable questions about what and where they are. Thus I have been proposing that we replace the second statement by statements concerning image pictures and descriptions.[7]

We no longer need to go hunting for images any more than we need to go hunting for centaurs. Yet if a centaur happens to pass by some day, we can easily accommodate to that without much trouble, though if a mental image liberated itself and fell on the desk before me, I doubt if I could recognize it as such. What really matters is that we are not committed to there being any centaurs or images; but neither are we committed to there being none.

Finally, interpretations of image-talk along the lines suggested here throw a different light on cognitive psychology. Having an image amounts not to possessing some immaterial picture in something called a mind but to having and exercising certain skills—a matter of producing, judging, revising certain material pictures and descriptions. To Howard Gardner's statement that "in talking about human cognitive activities, it is necessary to speak about mental representations" perhaps we should add a clause: "but talk of mental representations turns out in the end to be talk of cognitive activities".

4. Clearing the Head

Ironically, the final paper in a conference on images and understanding[8] calls in question the whole notion of mental images as pictures in the mind. And despite my rather emphatic assurances that much ordinary and scientific discourse that is ostensibly about mental images can be significant and valid, the

---

7. Those who feel handicapped by being denied a license to talk as if there are images may still say there are images, provided that is understood as saying that at least someone has an image, and this is interpreted in the way outlined above.

8. See note 5 above.

physiologist, neurologist, and psychologist working on cognition may be somewhat dismayed. As a philosopher long allied with cognitive psychology, I am by no means condemning all that cognitive scientists say and do, but rather seeking clarification of some of it. Since talk of 'pictures in the mind' taken literally is nonsense, and taken metaphorically needs careful interpretation, it can be highly misleading.

An analogy may help here. We all have responsibilities, some of them more pressing than others. But to suppose that there are such things, such entities, as responsibilities is to risk utter confusion that can be avoided if we speak rather of being responsible for doing so-and-so, for acting in a certain way, and ask what this involves. Likewise, in an earlier discussion (*MM*, 21–28), I suggested that having a mental image may be construed in terms of ability to perform certain activities; for instance, I may be said to have a horse-image in my mind to the extent that I can describe or draw a horse, sort descriptions and pictures into those that are of horses and those that are not, criticize or revise faulty descriptions and pictures of horses.

When a physiologist says in effect that a certain image consists of a certain pattern of firings of cells in the cerebral cortex, he is reporting on painstaking scientific investigation. But how has he validated this formulation? Surely, by checking it not against pictures he finds and examines in the brain but against verbal reports and other behavior of the subject. Such a physiological account and the sort of philosophical account I have outlined are complementaries. Putting them together we get, with some ellipsis, something roughly like this: when firings of the required kind occur in certain cells, the subject can to some extent produce, sort out, criticize, revise descriptions or pictures of a horse. The 'image' and the 'picture in the mind' have vanished; mythical inventions have been beneficially excised. Of course, in less formal discourse we may speak loosely of mental images or pictures so long as we remain aware that such talk is dangerous and needs careful interpretation. Its dangers and the difficulties of inter-

preting it increase when, as in talk of rotation and other manipulation of mental images, the context becomes more complex. As
Roger Shepard fully recognizes,[9] we must construe informal talk
of rotating images in some way that does not imply that there
are images twirling in the head.

Thus while a conviction that, literally, there are no pictures in
the head may challenge some work in psychology, it is entirely
compatible with the pursuit of cognitive science.[10]

(*Goodman*)

9. In a postscript prepared for a volume based on the "Images and Understanding"
conference.

10. I have profited from Robert Schwartz's brilliant "Imagery—There's More to It
Than Meets the Eye", *PSA 1980*, 2, ed. P. D. Asquith and R. N. Giere (East Lansing:
Philosophy of Science Association, 1981), pp. 285–301.

VI

Inertia and Invention

The terms "convention" and "conventional" are flagrantly and intricately ambiguous. On the one hand, the conventional is the ordinary, the usual, the traditional, the orthodox as against the novel, the deviant, the unexpected, the heterodox. On the other hand, the conventional is the artificial, the invented, the optional as against the natural, the fundamental, the mandatory. Thus we may have unconventional conventions (unusual artifices) and conventional nonconventions (familiar facts). The two uses of "convention" are not only different but almost opposite—yet not quite so; for to say that something is usual carries some suggestion that there are less usual alternatives; and what is mandatory, without alternatives, is usual.

1. The Optional

Philosophers have been primarily concerned with convention as fabricated form imposed on uninterpreted content. Sometimes they aim at clearing away artifice to discover pure fact, sometimes simply at distinguishing the contributions of convention and of content. But the conventional as the usual, the habitual, cannot be dismissed as merely a popular usage that occasions frequent confusion, for it plays a major role in some theoretical contexts. For instance, in a recent paper on literary theory, the author writes: "In this essay, 'conventions' refers to *manifestations of shared practices.*"[1] But I shall begin by considering convention as contrasted with content, the conventional as the optional or artificial as contrasted with the mandatory or factual.

Consider the motion of the moon. The moon rotates in that its orientation to the sun changes in a certain regular way, but it is fixed on its axis in that its orientation to the earth never changes. Does it rotate or not, then? Well, yes and no. If that seems self-contradictory, we like to say that the moon rotates relative to the sun but not relative to the earth. But this is a somewhat deceptive way of speaking; for to say that something 'moves relative to' something else is not to impute any motion to it at all. To say that the moon rotates relative to the sun is entirely compatible with saying that the sun revolves around a fixed moon. And to say that the moon does not rotate relative to the earth is entirely compatible with the earth's revolving around a rotating moon, as well as with saying that both the earth and moon remain at rest. So perhaps, to avoid giving a false impression, one should say simply that different aspects of the moon face the sun at different times; and that the same aspect of the moon faces the earth at all times. No more about rotation, rest, revolution; no more indeed about motion. Motion disappears from the realm of fact. And that should have been expected from the start, when the question "Does the moon rotate or not?" is answered by "That depends upon what we take as frame of reference". It depends upon what we do; we *make* the moon rotate or stand still. Motion

1. Steven Mailloux, "Rhetorical Hermeneutics", *Critical Inquiry* 11 (1985) 638, n. 5.

is optional, a matter of convention, of fabrication imposed upon what we find.

2. The Mandatory

But, then, what *is* found? The size and shape of the moon vary, it seems, according to the speed and direction of its motion. Thus since motion is a matter of convention, so are size and shape, and these also must be subtracted from fact. And of course any description in terms of the sun, moon, earth, and so on is conventional in that there are alternative equally legitimate versions in terms of other concepts. Organization into these familiar units, like the organization of stars into constellations, is optional (*MM*, 40–42). All fact threatens to evaporate into convention, all nature into artifice.

You are not likely to go along with this, but to protest: "How can there be no fact, no content, but only alternative ways of describing nothing? Surely there must be something that is described, however many different ways there are of describing it. There must be some line between what there is and how we describe it."

Quite so. The two statements about the moon are alternatives in that they describe something in common: in that they are about the same objects; agree with certain observations, measurements, and principles; and are in some way descriptive of the same facts. Yet these objects, observations, measurements, principles are themselves conventional; these facts are creatures of their descriptions. Two versions are 'of the same facts' to the extent that they share some terms, comprise some identical or kindred concepts, can be translated into one another. All convention depends upon fact, yet all fact is convention.

3. The Optional Distinction

Is the distinction between convention and fact, then, indispensable but meaningless? Rather, I think *the distinction is itself con-*

ventional. That, of course, is meaningless if the distinction between convention and fact is meaningless. And if all facts are conventions and all conventions are facts, how can the distinction be meaningful, expecially for a hard-boiled extensionalist?

Consider for a moment the terms "immediate predecessor" and "immediate successor" as applied to the integers, or to the clockwise series of minute-marks on a watch face. Every integer, or every mark, is both an immediate predecessor and an immediate successor, yet the distinction between "immediate predecessor" and "immediate successor" does not vanish. For they are not categorical terms sorting a realm into different classes, but relational terms. So also for the terms "rest" and "motion". They do not sort bodies into classes; all bodies are at rest and in motion. And so also for "conventional" and "factual". They do not sort statements or versions into classes but relate versions to each other.

In other words, two terms that apply to exactly the same things may have parallel compounds that apply to very different things. The pairs of terms just discussed are cases of what I have elsewhere explained as difference in meaning through difference in secondary extensions. Although all centaurs are unicorns and all unicorns are centaurs, simply because there are no centaurs and no unicorns, still "centaurs" and "unicorns" differ in meaning in that certain parallel compounds of them are not coextensive; for example, not all centaur pictures (or descriptions)—indeed very few—are also unicorn pictures or descriptions (*PP*, 221–238). Likewise, while "immediate predecessor" and "immediate successor" are coextensive because both apply to all integers, still "immediate predecessor of the integer 5" and "immediate successor of the integer 5" name very different things. Again, while all bodies are both in motion and at rest, "moves relative to the earth" and "is at rest relative to the earth" do not apply to all the same things. And while "factual" and "conventional" are coextensive, applying to all versions, "factual relative to version *V*" and "conventional relative to version *V*" are not.

If we are asked under what circumstances an integer is immediate successor to another, we can readily reply that the immediate successor is that integer plus one. But if we are asked to explain under what circumstances one of two bodies moves relative to another, we may say, for the sun and the earth for example, "If the sun is fixed, the earth moves; if the sun moves, the earth is fixed". But the apparent conditionalization in the two clauses is specious. Compare such sentences as "If the black horse wins, I'm rich; if the white horse wins, I'm broke", where each antecedent is true or false according to which horse wins. In contrast, since unrelativized statements of motion are incomplete, the antecedents "the sun is fixed" and "the sun moves" are vacuous. We cannot determine whether the earth moves or is fixed by finding out whether the sun is fixed or moves; for the sun and the earth and all other bodies are both fixed and moving. A slightly different, familiar formulation runs: "On the assumption that the sun is fixed, the earth moves; on the assumption that the sun moves, the earth is fixed". Plainly, this is no better; for the 'assumptions', like the antecedents before, are vacuous. All this may not dispel a dogged conviction that nevertheless, in some sense or other, if the sun is taken as fixed, the earth moves; while if the sun is taken as moving, the earth is fixed. Putting it this way may seem to be going from bad to worse. For what does "taken as" mean? We cannot take hold of the sun or the earth and keep it still or give it a push to get it moving. And how can taking one body as fixed or moving make another revolve or stop? But when "taken as" is read as "plotted as" (under a given system) and associated adjustments are made, we have something like "When the sun is plotted as a point, the earth is to be plotted as a surrounding closed curve; when the sun is plotted as a closed curve, the earth is to be plotted as a surrounded point". "Plotting" may be broadened here to include mathematical or verbal descriptions. The faults of our former proposals vanish. Apparent talk of motion turns out to be talk of diagrams, descriptions, mathematical functions, versions.

Diagrams or other versions under a given system differing only through what is taken as fixed are alternatives, optional, conventional. Furthermore, a system of plotting whereby whatever is taken as fixed is shown as a point, and whatever is taken as moving is shown as a path, is itself conventional—one among alternative systems, each admitting various versions.

4. Stance

But what has become of 'the facts'? What are all these versions versions of? You may feel like the inspector in the television series who tires of talk and keeps insisting "Just the facts, ma'am!" But all that can be done to comply with a demand to say what the versions are versions of is to give another version. Each version tells what 'the facts' are; but the several versions are at odds with each other. How can the earth at the same time stand still, revolve around the sun, and move in countless other ways? How can divergent diagrams or versions be of the same objects, the same world? They must either be of no world or of different worlds. There must be many worlds if any.

That may suggest to you that we have taken leave, if not of our wits, at least of everyday experience and ordinary discourse. Let's get back to solid ground. A friend of mine was stopped by an officer of the law for driving fifty-six miles an hour. She argued, "But officer, taking the car ahead of me as fixed, I was not moving at all." "Never mind that," replied the officer, "You were going fifty-six miles an hour along the road, and," stamping his foot, "this is what is fixed." "Oh, come now, officer; surely you learned in school that this road as part of the earth is not fixed at all but is rotating rapidly eastward on its axis. Since I was driving westward, I was going slower than those cars parked over there." "O.K., lady, I'll give them all tickets for speeding right now— and you get a ticket for parking on the highway."

Where does this leave us? If everything is the way it is taken to be, and anything can be correctly taken in all sorts of opposing ways, are we condemned to chaos? No. For despite Bruno, and the speeder's sophistry, the officer was of course right in the first place. Although nothing is absolutely fixed or moving, and although whether it is fixed or how it moves depends upon how it is taken, that in turn depends upon context, circumstances, purpose. Where cars on the highway are concerned, the earth is taken as fixed, and the ticket for speeding is deserved. In other contexts, the earth is rotating and revolving; we use an alternative version.

Almost always, some *stance* or other is adopted. Merely noting that many alternative versions can be constructed does not provide us with any. We have to hold some things steady for a while as a working basis. Along with the recognition that there is no *fixed* distinction between fact and convention must go the recognition that nevertheless there is almost always *some* distinction or other between fact and convention—a transient distinction drawn by the stance adopted at the time. Adoption of a stance, as we have seen, turns a relational term into a categorial one; designation of an integer as origin divides the class of integers into origin, an immediate predecessor, an immediate successor, and all other integers; designation of certain bodies as fixed may sort other bodies into the fixed and the moving; designation of certain statements as mandatory may classify other statements as mandatory or optional. A shift in stance effects a re-sorting. The Copernican revolution constituted such a shift. It no more changed cosmology to fit the facts than it transformed the facts by changing stance from earth to sun.

Although a stance may be taken anywhere, and shifted often and without notice, it is not arbitrary. Most of our stances and shifts of stance are habitual, instilled by practice. We commonly take the earth as fixed in describing the motion of a plane, but on an airplane we automatically take the plane as fixed in describing the motion of the cabin crew. Where a choice of stance is more deliberate, it may involve complex considerations of simplicity, convenience, suitability to context, efficacy for a purpose, and accessibility by those we must communicate with. Taking the tip of a fly's wing as fixed in describing the motion of bodies in the solar system would presumably fail on all these counts.

5. Paradox

In sum, I have been urging such obvious points as that there is no firm distinction between fact and convention but that that distinction is very important; that the line between fact and convention shifts often and may be drawn anywhere but is not capricious; that when a convention (as option) becomes a convention (as the usual) it thus tends to become factual; and that rather than the facts determining how we take them, how we take them determines the facts—but that we had better be careful how we take them.

In a recent review of Italo Calvino's novel *Mr. Palomar*, Michael Wood puts it more poignantly:

A fact is what won't go away, what we cannot *not* know, as Henry James remarked of the real. Yet when we bring one closer, stare at it, test our loyalty to it, it begins to shimmer with complication. Without becoming less factual, it floats off into myth. Mr. Palomar looks at the sky, the lawn, the sea, a girl, giraffes, and much more. He wants only to observe, to learn a modest lesson from creatures and things. But he can't. There is too much to see in them, for a start. . . And there is too much of himself and his culture in the world he watches anyway: the world is littered with signs of our needs, with mythologies.[2]

Readers wanting more particular applications of what I have been saying should have no trouble working some out. Getting the facts straight is easy enough so long as we bear in mind that the facts are paradoxical.

(*Goodman*)

2. Michael Wood, "Theory with a Wife", *London Review of Books* 7 (October 3, 1985) 17.

VII

Confronting Novelty

1. Encounters of Two Kinds

Although many philosophical dualisms have been debunked, the dualism of nature and convention continues to haunt discussions of representation. Pictorial representation is thought to be natural—a matter of resemblance between image and object. This resemblance, moreover, is taken to be an objective matter, visible to the human eye and evident to all who look. Linguistic representation, on the other hand, is considered conventional—working by rules and stipulations that secure the connection between words and the world.

The bifurcation of symbols into the natural and the conventional is not without difficulties. A number of symbols, including star charts, hieroglyphics, and Chinese pictographs, seem intermediate cases. It is not clear whether they should be considered natural or conventional signs. Indeed, the criteria for classifying signs as natural or conventional are themselves obscure. The distinction is more easily formulated than applied. Still, it is not my purpose here to mount a frontal assault on the dichotomy. In fact it is widely accepted. And once it is accepted, theorists have reason to limit their inquiries. Since the conventional is patently different from the natural, theorists concerned with the one can safely ignore representations belonging to the other. As a result, affinities between the two realms are often overlooked, and differences—because anticipated—unheeded. If, however, we abandon the presumption that theories of linguistic and pictorial representation are mutually irrelevant, the results of each can be taken to bear on the other. Then neglected affinities can be recognized, and acknowledged differences rendered salient. This, I hope, will enhance our understanding of representations of all sorts.

I want to concentrate on a single problem that is shared by linguistics and the theory of depiction: the problem of explaining our ability to understand representations we have not previously encountered. We regularly comprehend sentences we've never before heard and pictures we've never before seen. Our competence, of course, has its limits. Sentences that are mumbled, garbled, or in an alien tongue, like pictures that are out of focus, poorly executed, or in an unfamiliar style, are apt to elude us. Still, our failures may be less troublesome than our successes. If the ability to interpret symbols depends on experience, then lack of experience with a particular symbol seems readily to account for failure to understand it. Not so readily explained, however, is the wide range of symbols that are understood without difficulty despite lack of experience with them. Whether or not our capacity to interpret symbols depends on experience, it plainly extends beyond experience. The problem is to say how.

Although the problem is common to linguistics and art theory, the solution is thought not to be. Central to each discipline is an account of competence that cannot plausibly apply to the representations of the other. Linguistic representation is taken to depend on rules. These rules, being general, settle the interpretation of novel as well as familiar expressions. Pictorial representation is taken to depend on likeness. Since likeness can be seen directly, no prior acquaintance with the pictorial symbols is required to understand a picture. Words, manifestly, do not resemble their objects. So the theory of pictorial competence cannot be true of linguistic competence. And we have neither grammars nor lexicons of pictorial forms, so linguistic theory cannot account for pictorial competence. Still, the problem deserves more attention, for the mutual indifference of linguistics and art theory is such that the relation between the two competences is not taken to be in the province of either. Moreover, the mutual indifference of the disciplines is not argued for; it is simply given in the demarcation of the subjects. So any relevance of theories in the one discipline to problems in the other is apt to be unnoticed.

2. Linguistic Competence

Contemporary theorists[1] contend that linguistic competence consists in the mind's having and being able to use a lexicon and a grammar. The mental lexicon determines the meanings of individual words; the mental grammar determines how the meanings of significant strings of words derive from the meanings of their constituents. The mind is thought to be, or to be closely analogous to, a digital computer; the lexicon and the grammar, part of the program; interpretation, a type of data processing. We understand a sentence we have never before heard because its words are contained in our lexicon, its form in our grammar. We thus already know the meanings of the individual words and the rule for obtaining the meaning of the whole from the meanings of the parts. To interpret the sentence, we simply apply the rule to the words. We do exactly the same in interpreting familiar sentences.

This account has a certain appeal, for it models inaccessible internal processes on familiar public activities. When confronted

---

1. Cf. Noam Chomsky, *Aspects of the Theory of Syntax* (Cambridge, Mass.: MIT Press, 1965); and Jerry Fodor, *The Language of Thought* (New York: Thomas Y. Crowell, 1975).

with an English sentence we don't understand, we consult grammar books and dictionaries. Often the information they contain
settles the interpretation straightaway. Morever, consulting such
works may be the only general method we have for interpreting
problematic sentences. Why not assume that the same sort of
process occurs naturally in the interpretation of unproblematic
sentences? Only in these cases, the process is effortless, instan-
taneous, and unconscious. For the requisite grammatical and lexical information is already stored in the mind.

In learning a foreign language, we may memorize vocabulary
lists and grammatical rules. This seems extraordinarily like attempting to supply ourselves with an internal lexicon and grammar for the language.[2] Moreover, in the early stages, we may
explicitly appeal to the rules and lists to generate interpretations
of sentences. As we gain fluency, conscious appeal to the rules
and lists we have learned occurs less often. Perhaps, however,
the process of interpretation does not fundamentally change. We
simply internalize the vocabulary lists and grammatical rules and
so come to apply them without thinking.

One final attraction of this picture of linguistic competence is
that we know how computers work. So if the human mind is,
or is analogous to, a computer, we can use our knowledge of
computers to learn about ourselves. A good deal of research in
the cognitive sciences is grounded in the conviction that the computer is a model of the mind. Indeed, according to Jerry Fodor,[3]
it's the only model of the mind we've got.

The appeal of this account stems from analogies to overt linguistic or quasilinguistic activities. But they are only analogies.
Interpreting unproblematic sentences in our native tongue in-

2. Contemporary linguists do not believe that this is how fundamental grammatical
and lexical information is acquired. My point here is that the appeal of the account
to nonlinguists may stem from such analogies.

3. Jerry Fodor, "Methodological Solipsism Considered as a Research Strategy in
Cognitive Psychology", in *Representations* (Cambridge, Mass.: MIT Press, 1983), pp.
225-253.

volves no conscious consultation of an internal grammar or lexicon. Nor does introspection reveal any such activity. Proponents of the view under consideration admit that accessing the internal code is a deeply unconscious process. The reason to believe that it occurs is that it is embedded in a powerful linguistic theory. We should believe that speakers 'access' an internal syntactic and semantic code for the same reason that we believe that distant bodies are drawn together by gravitational attraction—because the theses are supported by powerful, comprehensive, general, explanatory theories. Still, it is important to notice that the linguistic theory receives no direct support from a speaker's own sense of how he understands what is said.

Moreover, the competences we are said to have at the unconscious level are not competences we have at the conscious level. We typically cannot state the grammatical rules for our own language, or give the meanings of our terms. Nevertheless, we speak grammatically and meaningfully. Perhaps, as the linguists suggest, we do so because deep down we know the requisite grammatical and lexical rules. Or perhaps we do so because neither deep nor superficial knowledge of such rules is needed for meaningful, grammatical speech.

The case of meaning is particularly telling. Sameness of meaning seemingly involves more than coextensiveness of terms; but satisfiable, intuitively adequate standards for synonymy have not been found.[4] Since the internal lexicon is said to contain the meanings of our terms, the unclarity surrounding the notion of meaning results in an unclarity about what information the lexicon is supposed to contain. Minimally, it seems, this much is required: the lexical entry for a term should constitute a criterion for the term's application. Criteria for the applicability of terms are as difficult to articulate as meanings. On the broadest construal, such a criterion is adequate if it allows for the application of a term to

4. W. V. Quine, "Two Dogmas of Empiricism", in *From a Logical Point of View* (Cambridge, Mass.: Harvard University Press, 1961), pp. 20–46.

all and only the items in the term's extension. Even if we require no more than this, the internal lexicon does not measure up.

Often nothing in the mind of the speaker determines the extension of his terms. I may know that "Feynman" and "Gell-Mann" name eminent physicists, but know nothing that distinguishes one from the other. And I may know that "beech" and "elm" designate separate classes of deciduous trees, but have no idea how to tell them apart. My linguistic competence is not imperiled by my ignorance, for I normally use the terms in contexts where the differences do not matter, and I know enough, when the situation warrants, to defer to members of the linguistic community who possess the knowledge I lack.[5] Moreover, the knowledge in question is not primarily linguistic. In the one case it is biographical; in the other botanical.

Fodor concedes this point[6] and concludes that the lexicon is referentially opaque. Its entries determine the concepts we think in, but not what we think about. The lexical entry for "elm" then yields an elm-concept. And this concept is involved in our elm-thoughts. But since the concept is opaque, there is no reason to think that it determines the extension of "elm".

The analogy between minds and computers is illuminating here. For computer simulations are strictly ambiguous, having a referential and a computational interpretation. Under the former, a computer simulation represents, say, a complex molecular interaction. Under the latter, it defines a sequence of states of the computer. The former enables the scientist to interpret it as a representation of physical reality; the latter enables the machine to perform its calculations. The computer, of course, knows nothing of the referential interpretation. Moreover, its capacity to com-

5. Saul Kripke, "Naming and Necessity", in *Semantics of Natural Language*, ed. Donald Davidson and Gilbert Harman (Dordrecht: D. Reidel, 1972), p. 292; Hilary Putnam, "The Meaning of 'Meaning'", in *Mind, Language, and Reality* (Cambridge: Cambridge University Press, 1975), pp. 245–246.

6. Fodor, "Tom Swift and His Procedural Grandmother", in *Representations*, pp. 204–224.

pile and execute its program would not be enhanced if the referential interpretation could somehow be imparted to it. To perform its calculations, the computer requires only the computational interpretation: the specification of its original state and of the changes it undergoes in response to various commands. The fact that the program has another interpretation that maps the operations and results onto physical reality is computationally irrelevant.

Correspondingly, if all we knew about the computer simulation was the interpretation available to the computer, we would not know that it represents a molecular interaction. (Indeed, we would not know that it represents at all.) But, according to Fodor, this is precisely our situation with respect to the sentences we comprehend. The internal lexicon is the machine language of the human computer. It yields computational interpretations that enable us to use sentences in our reasoning. But it does not yield referential interpretations, for lexical entries are opaque. Thus the information about the sentence that the lexicon provides does not determine what the sentence represents. Questions concerning the truth value of the sentence or the referents of its terms are inappropriate on a computational reading. Fodor's theory can explain neither how we know what novel sentences represent nor how we know what familiar sentences represent.[7] (Indeed, if his account is correct, it is surprising that we know such things.) The role of the lexicon has evolved to serve other purposes.

There is another limitation on the linguists' account: it cannot explain our understanding of figurative language or of locutions in which grammatical rules are deliberately violated. Understanding a stream-of-consciousness work, for example, is not a matter of forcing on it an interpretation that accords with our ordinary grammatical conventions or their 'deep structure' counterparts.

---

7. Fodor uses the term "representation" somewhat differently. He takes the computational interpretation to be a representation. I restrict the term to interpretations under which a symbol is a symbol *of* something. As I use the term, only when functioning referentially do symbols represent.

For the work achieves its effect not in spite of, but because of, its odd, ungrammatical constructions. To force a grammatical reading on the work is to miss the point.

Typically the objects a term applies to metaphorically are not in the term's literal extension. Nor does the metaphorical usage play the same computational role as the literal usage. In calling Wilbur a workhorse, we liken the man to literal workhorses. The metaphor suggests that, like literal workhorses, he is plodding, diligent, but perhaps a bit uninspired. And understanding the metaphor involves picking up on some of these (or related) suggestions. It also involves recognizing that Wilbur is not said to be in the literal extension of the term "workhorse". So some of the predicates of literal workhorses—"quadruped", "herbivore", and the like—are not being ascribed to Wilbur. Since the lexicon is the repository of literal meanings exclusively, it follows that the lexical counterpart of the term "workhorse" enters into computations or inferences that are invalid when the term is used metaphorically. For instance, the literal reading permits, and the metaphorical reading prohibits, the inference:

If x is a workhorse, x is a quadruped.

It cannot plausibly be maintained that the metaphorical meaning of a term is contained along with its literal meaning in the lexicon. For there are potentially indefinitely many metaphorical applications of a given term. The term "workhorse", for example, might be applied to automobiles—picking out jeeps and other such vehicles. Not only does its reference change as the term is applied metaphorically to sort different realms, so does its computational role. Inferences like

If x is a workhorse, x is dull

or

If x is a workhorse, x is uninspired

might be allowed when the term "workhorse" is applied meta-

phorically to people, but not (at least not under their literal interpretations) when it is applied to cars. In that application, however,

If x is a workhorse, x is capable of pulling heavy loads

is allowable, although we would not accept such an inference
(literally construed) about human workhorses.

It will not do for linguists to dismiss such cases as deviant—
to contend that metaphorical sentences are strictly false, and
stream-of-consciousness locutions strictly ill-formed. For even if
this were true, it would be irrelevant. Whether we characterize
them as true or false, as well-formed or ill-formed, we understand
such sequences of words. And linguistics claims to explain our
comprehension of and competence with words. Although sustained systematic violations of grammatical rules are relatively
rare, they are often not hard to understand. That being so, it is
reasonable to expect the theory of linguistic comprehension to
explain how we understand them. An account that applies only
to cases in which our standards of grammaticality are met seems
seriously incomplete. Moreover, metaphors are ubiquitous. So
the failure of linguistic theory to explain our understanding of
sentences containing metaphors is a failure to explain a consid-
erable proportion of its subject matter.

What remains is an impoverished notion of linguistic competence. Knowledge of word-world connections, and understanding
of nonliteral and nongrammatical uses of words, are excluded
from linguistic comprehension. (Conceivably these are cases of,
or are involved in, comprehension of some other sort.) Surely
they are involved in understanding sentences we've never heard
before. For example, to understand the sentence

Descartes is the Robinson Crusoe of the mind

I need to know something about who Descartes is and what he
accomplished, about who the fictional character Robinson Crusoe
is and the story in which he appears, about how fictive terms
can be applied metaphorically to characterize actual individuals,

and about how a proper name prefaced by an article functions metaphorically as a general term. Since I have the requisite knowledge, I have no difficulty understanding the sentence the first time I hear it. It seems somewhat eccentric to maintain that my understanding is not linguistic, for it is surely grounded in an appreciation of how the words in the sentence function.

3. Pictorial Competence

The linguists' model plainly cannot be extended to pictorial comprehension. Lexicons and grammars are possible only for systems whose symbols are determinate and discriminable. For lexicons and grammars consist of generalizations that apply to symbols because they are tokens of specific syntactic types. Where it is impossible to determine the type a symbol belongs to, it is impossible to take it to be subject to lexical and grammatical rules. And where it is impossible to tell whether two symbols belong to the same type, it is impossible to treat them as syntactically interchangeable.

But this is precisely the situation with regard to pictorial symbols. For such symbols belong to systems that are syntactically dense.[8] There is no way to differentiate pictorial symbols sharply from one another, hence no way to determine which symbol a particular mark belongs to or whether two marks belong to the same symbol. Any difference among pictorial marks might be syntactically significant. And for pictorial systems there is no principled basis for ruling that certain differences among marks are irrelevant (*LA*, 130–141). Understanding a picture, then, is not a matter of bringing to bear universal rules that determine the identification and manipulation of its component symbols.

That the linguist's solution is inapplicable to pictorial representations may be unimportant. For perhaps pictures belong to a realm in which the linguist's problem does not arise. It might

8. But see Chapter VIII below.

be argued that determinate, satisfiable rules are required for the interpretation of linguistic representations because the connection between word and object is not naturally secured. Then, if there is a natural connection between pictures and their subjects, this obviates the need for grammatical and lexical rules of pictorial representation.[9] Resemblance is often held to be that connection.[10]

The argument goes roughly as follows: We know what a picture represents because we recognize its resemblance to its subject. This resemblance, moreover, is discernible to the uneducated eye. If it were not, we could not tell what a picture represents just by looking. But we do that all the time; we regularly understand pictures we've never seen before.

Manifestly, resemblance is not sufficient for representation. For representation is asymmetric; resemblance, symmetric. A picture represents its subject; that subject does not represent the picture. But the subject resembles the picture as much and in the same ways as the picture resembles the subject. Moreover, many items that resemble one another do not represent one another. Identical twins are typically not each other's stand-ins (*LA*, 3–5). Still, where we know on other grounds that something is a representation, perhaps it is on the basis of resemblance that we determine what it represents.

Resemblance may be as difficult a notion as meaning, but for a different reason. Whereas meanings are elusive, resemblances are ubiquitous. Any two objects resemble each other in some respect. The problem is to specify the sort of resemblance that is required for pictorial representation.

The obvious answer is: visual resemblance. Although obvious, this answer is not obviously right. We often know what a picture represents without knowing (or caring) whether it resembles its subject. Crucifixion being an outmoded method of public exe-

9. C. S. Peirce, *Selected Papers*, ed. Philip Wiener (New York: Dover, 1958), pp. 368, 391.

10. Alan Tormey, "Seeing Things: Pictures, Paradox and Perspective", *Perceiving Artworks*, ed. John Fisher (Philadelphia: Temple University Press, 1980), pp. 59–75.

cution, we do not know whether pictures of Christ's crucifixion look like the real thing. Nevertheless, we can typically tell straightaway what those pictures represent.

Moreover, pictures with fictional subjects do not resemble their referents. Unicorn pictures do not resemble unicorns, there being none to resemble. Still, we have little difficulty recognizing unicorn pictures for what they are. Whatever enables us to comprehend such pictures, it cannot be resemblance of a representation to its denotation. The denotation of a unicorn picture is null, and so is identical to the denotation of a centaur picture. But we are unlikely to mistake the subject of the one for the subject of the other.

To be sure, many pictures resemble their subjects. If resemblance can be shown to explain how we understand these pictures, perhaps a way can be found to extend the explanation to more problematic cases. But even the seemingly clear cases raise difficulties. For pictures can resemble their subjects in any number of ways. Successful impressionist works capture fleeting, ephemeral properties of changing visible surfaces—shimmering juxtapositions of sunlight and shadow that are taken in at a glance and gone in a flash. Pictures on the walls of Egyptian tombs are schematic representations of the ineluctable cycle of the seasons. In their changelessness and generality, the pictures represent and resemble the eternal and unalterable order of nature.[11] The evanescent moment that the impressionist captures is an instant in the eternal cycle that the Egyptian records.

Any thing looks many ways. So to contend that a picture looks like its subject is not to specify a particular relation between the two. Pictures that resemble the same thing may look very different from one another. And pictures that look very much alike may represent quite different things.

Indeed, pictures that resemble their subjects do not always

11. E. H. Gombrich, *Art and Illusion* (Princeton: Princeton Unversity Press, 1969), pp. 122–125.

resemble the ways their subjects look. In medieval paintings, for example, the images of the madonna and child are often significantly bigger than the images of the saints that surround them. According to the religious tradition within which these works were produced, the infant Jesus and his mother are far more significant than other people. And size in such pictures is a measure of religious significance. To represent the Christ child as no greater than an ordinary baby would be incorrect. For in this system, pictorial magnitude is a measure of real (theological or metaphysical) magnitude, not of apparent (physical) magnitude.

This phenomenon is not peculiar to religious pictures. Scientific photographs—for example, x-rays and cloud chamber photographs—likewise do not resemble the visible aspects of their subjects. They function, rather, to render visible what is normally invisible. Their images resemble features of their objects that are not directly seen.[12]

The thesis that pictorial competence is a matter of resemblance shares a weakness with the thesis that linguistic competence is a matter of rules: namely, the inablility to account for our comprehension of figurative symbols. Understanding a picture often involves knowing what its symbols represent figuratively as well as knowing what they represent literally. When a knight is depicted with a dog at his side, for example, the dog typically symbolizes loyalty. To understand the picture fully, we have to know both that the configuration on the canvas literally represents a dog and that, because it does, it metaphorically refers to loyalty. The dog image thus contributes to the pictorial representation of the knight as loyal. Many pictorial metaphors are more subtle. But whether the metaphor is subtle or stereotypical, knowing what the image resembles does not suffice for knowing how and what it represents.

Even where a picture bears a decided resemblance to its subject,

---

12. E. H. Gombrich, "Standards of Truth: The Arrested Image and the Moving Eye", *The Image and the Eye* (Ithaca: Cornell University Press, 1982), pp. 245–247.

we are not always able to discern that resemblance. Unless we know what to look for, what to focus on, what to overlook, we may fail to see a likeness that is right before our eyes. And such knowledge is not a native endowment, but a complex constellation of acquired abilities. Humans do not automatically see variegated pastel patches as mottled light and shadow. We learn to see that way in learning to understand impressionist painting. Nor is it intuitively obvious that figures in Egyptian paintings represent generally. The difference between the general and the particular, and the way that difference is captured pictorially, are things that have to be learned. And in different pictorial systems, different devices are used. These are not special cases. Learning is required even to recognize what photographs represent. As Gombrich notes, until relatively recently, unposed snapshots were incomprehensible.[13] And manifestly, a good deal of learning is required to be able to read x-ray photographs.

Recognition of what a picture resembles is sometimes a consequence of knowledge of what it represents. The experience of looking at photographs of other people's babies bears this out. In general, baby pictures look like babies. But it is not always obvious which picture resembles which baby. When we learn whose picture we're looking at, certain features may acquire a salience. We see the wide open eyes and the skeptical tilt of the chin as characteristic of Emily. The resemblance, we admit, is remarkable, even though it was not in fact remarked until we learned the identity of the picture's subject.

Similarly, it is often easier to discern the subject of a cubist painting after reading the caption. I have no trouble finding an image of a woman with a guitar, once I know what to look for. And I recognize that, in its way, the image resembles a woman with a guitar. But I might never have seen it, had I not known it was there.

Sometimes the identification of the subject of a picture occasions

13. Gombrich, "Standards of Truth", p. 273.

a reinterpretation of the work. What once looked to be a beatific smile on the face of an apostle becomes a malevolent sneer when the apostle is identified as Judas. This can occur for figurative symbols as well. The dog that was taken to be a symbol of loyalty is reconstrued as an ironic symbol of treachery when the knight beside him is recognized as King Arthur's faithless knight, Mordred (*LA*, 83).

Resemblance turns out to be a red herring. Its apprehension does not assure, nor its absence preclude, understanding what a picture represents. Moreover, resemblance does not designate a single relation between pictures and their subjects; it designates the members of a fairly comprehensive class of relations—a class whose boundaries are not clear. And relations of resemblance are not always immediately evident to the uneducated eye. Knowing how to look at a picture is required to discern the ways it resembles its subject, just as it is required to discern other pictorial properties. Knowledge of other matters may be required as well— pictorial conventions; referential connections; historical, scientific, or mythical lore that sets the context of the work. Such matters are not taken in in a glance.

To deny that resemblance is the basis for pictorial representation is not to say that anything can be a picture of anything else. There may well be limits on the structure and complexity of systems we can master. And some systems may be more easily mastered than others. But ease of mastery may have little to do with estimations of pictorial likeness. Illustrations in picture books and Saturday morning cartoons are among the earliest pictures children master. They are not, however, thought to be particularly accurate likenesses of their objects.

Pictures are ubiquitous. A child in our culture is likely to encounter them on billboards, posters, and packages; on the walls of the buildings he frequents; in books, comic strips, and cartoons. He is likely to begin to learn to identify pictures at the same time and in the same ways as he learns to identify other things. He is taught to recognize dog pictures and house pictures, just as he is taught to recognize dogs and houses. Learning to comprehend pictures often occurs in the context of learning about other things. The child who learns to differentiate horses from zebras by looking at their pictures learns simultaneously to differentiate horse pictures from zebra pictures. The student who learns to recognize diseased organs by studying a medical text is also learning to interpret medical illustrations. In such cases, the occurrence of pictorial learning and the consequent development of pictorial competence are apt to be overlooked, since learning to interpret the pictures is a means to some other end.

That end can, of course, be achieved in other ways. Some children learn to recognize zebras by looking directly at zebras. And observant operating room technicians might learn to recognize liver disease by looking directly at diseased livers. But these people do not thereby acquire the correlated pictorial competence. Medical illustrations may remain unintelligible to the technicians, and animal pictures to the children. To use a picture to identify its subject or the subject to comprehend the picture requires understanding how the picture represents its subject. So even when its subject is familiar, a picture remains enigmatic to those who are ignorant of the relevant pictorial practices.

Pictorial learning involves acquiring a wide range of perceptual and conceptual skills and developing a sensitivity regarding their exercise. Pictures represent in many different ways. And different skills are needed to understand pictures of different kinds. But each system need not be learned from scratch. For pictorial learning also involves developing second-order skills. These enable us to modify and extend our interpretive abilities and so comprehend pictures in systems related to those we know. The viewer who is already adept at interpreting traditional realistic paintings is likely to have little difficulty learning to understand realistic works with multiple vanishing points.

Having mastered a pictorial system, we simply see what its pictures represent. The process is so nearly automatic that we are apt to forget that interpretation occurs. Deliberation is not normally required to understand what is represented in newspaper photographs or realistic drawings. So the failure of such pictures to conform to our expectations is disconcerting. A paradoxical drawing by Escher forcefully reminds us that pictures are two-dimensional surfaces on which we try to impose three-dimensional interpretations. And a photograph of the surface of Mars reminds us that the medium does not supply its own scale of size and distance. The frustration of our expectations thus highlights our cognitive contribution to pictorial interpretation. It brings to consciousness factors that are frequently overlooked.

4. Common Ground

Despite serious failings, the theory that linguistic competence depends on rules and the theory that pictorial competence depends on resemblances endures. Why? Primarily, I think, because of a dearth of plausible alternatives. And this in turn is explained by the conception of competence that the theories share. Both take the competence in question to be a general ability to comprehend symbols of a given kind on the basis of the syntax and semantics of the symbols exclusively. Given this conception of competence, it is hard to see how anything except universal rules or particular resemblances could serve.

But this conception of representational competence is itself questionable. Although we plainly have the ability to understand some representations we've never before encountered, we do not understand every English sentence we hear or every pictorial representation we see. A sentence from Henry James's *The Golden Bowl* or a picture like Manet's *Le Déjeuner sur l'Herbe* may elude understanding, despite the comprehensibility of the individual syntactic and semantic elements. We just don't know what to make of it.

Moreover, our understanding of representations often depends on knowledge that is not specifically syntactical or semantical. Such knowledge, we have seen, may be required to differentiate

Feynman from Gell-Mann, a beech from an elm, a smile from a sneer. These matters may need to be settled to determine just what a particular symbol represents. And such knowledge may be required to decide whether the representation of a dog in a picture or story is a symbol of loyalty, a symbol of treachery, or simply a symbol of a dog.

Interpretation of a symbol depends on its place in the various symbol systems it belongs to. And it depends on the systems available and appropriate for classifying the symbol itself.

A symbol system is a system of implicit alternatives that collectively sort the objects in a realm (*LA*, 72). And the same symbol can belong to several systems and so participate in a variety of sortings. The extension of "fish", for example, sometimes includes, sometimes excludes shellfish. And the truth values of many sentences about fish vary depending on which system is in play. "All fish are vertebrates" is true under the narrow interpretation, false under the broad interpretation of the term. But many other sentences are indifferent as between the two readings. "Fish are aquatic", and "Fish are a good source of protein" remain true under both interpretations. So an isolated sentence need not favor either one.

Similar things occur in pictorial representations. A single drawing might represent a trout, a rainbow trout, a steelhead. Differences in markings that exclude a fish from one of the classes that the drawing represents do not exclude it from another. To understand the picture in its various functions, we have to realize that in one system it excludes fish that aren't trout; in another it also excludes trout that aren't rainbow trout; and in another it also excludes rainbow trout that aren't steelheads.

Manifestly, the issue becomes even more complicated when the symbols have fictive or figurative applications in addition to, or instead of, literal, factual ones. Often a symbol belongs to several systems, and we need to know which and how many of them it is functioning in to understand what and how it represents.

Symbols are themselves subject to classification. And understanding a representation involves knowing some of the ways it is classified. We classify representations by subject, as crucifixion pictures or medical bulletins; by style, as impressionist paintings or symbolist poems; by genre, as still lifes or short stories. And we classify them by medium, as watercolors or news reports; by author, as Monets or Flauberts; by historical and cultural milieu, as Renaissance or Victorian works. There is no obvious limit to the knowledge of a representation and its context that could, in principle, enhance our understanding of it.

These points do not pertain exclusively to works of art. To understand a newspaper article, for example, we need to classify it as a news report, a feature, a column, or an editorial. We do well to know whether it was subject to military censorship or to editorial policies that restrict what is said or the way it is said. And we need to know the systems of alternatives to which its terms belong. In calling a country a friendly power, do we exclude only such regimes as are actually belligerent to us, or all those that do not actively support our interests? Although we do not ordinarily deliberate about them, appreciation of such matters forms the background against which our reading of the news makes sense.

This threatens to make our original problem intractable, taking so much to be relevant to the interpretation of a symbol that understanding a representation seems a remarkable achievement, not an everyday occurrence. The resulting richness and complexity of symbols is hard to square with our ordinary unsophisticated comprehension of pictures and sentences.

The worry rests on a pair of related misconceptions: the first is the conviction that understanding a symbol is an all-or-nothing affair; the second, that a symbol has a single, uniquely correct interpretation. Ascertaining that interpretation is then necessary and sufficient for understanding the symbol. Nothing less will do, and nothing more is needed to understand what a symbol represents.

But understanding admits of degrees. A little knowledge of a symbol and its context can yield some small understanding of what the symbol represents. We recognize that the pronoun "he" and a conventional stick figure represent a male even though we cannot identify him further. The greater our store of relevant knowledge, the greater our resources for (and hence, prospects of) understanding what the symbol represents. Moreover, the growth of understanding may involve the recognition of several admissible alternative interpretations and may occasion the reconsideration of some we have already accepted. A symbol that had been construed literally is reconstrued metaphorically, sometimes revoking the literal reading, sometimes augmenting it. Or several separate literal readings are identified.

To be sure, some modes of representation are so simple and familiar that understanding is easily achieved. But even here the understanding may be illusory or incomplete. An apparent compliment contains a hidden slight; a passing remark, a manifestation of deep-seated resentment. Psychoanalysts and critics have shown that even seemingly simple representations contain significantly more than a superficial reading reveals.

In understanding a representation, as in understanding anything else, we use the cognitive resources we have, realizing that they may be inadequate. We bring to the task of interpreting an unfamiliar picture or sentence the background of related representations we already understand, along with any additional knowledge and skill we can press into service. Often these suffice. If not, then by modifying and extending our previous understanding we can sometimes arrive at an adequate interpretation. But not always. No rules or relations guarantee that a correct interpretation will be achieved. There are no recipes.

(*Elgin*)

VIII

Representation Re-presented

Representation in the sense of depiction[1] is a complicated matter—just how complicated I am only now beginning to realize. Once we free ourselves from the dogma that depiction can be defined as reference by a symbol to something it resembles, we face the hard task of finding a more adequate characterization. In *Languages of Art* one rather complex condition was suggested as perhaps necessary but by no means sufficient. Since then I have come to an increasingly deeper understanding of even that condition—as well as of the difficulties of arriving at a sufficient condition and, indeed, of the whole problem of depiction.

1. Answers

Almost everyone knows that the difference between a picture of Paris and a name or description of it is that the picture is more

1. "Representation" is an especially ambiguous term. In *Languages of Art* it is used specifically for pictorial representation. I now prefer to call this *depiction*, leaving "representation" for looser and more flexible use.

like the city. That, of course, is nonsense; likeness is neither required nor enough for depiction. The word "word" is much like the word "world" and denotes that word, along with every other, but is still no picture of that word; and a postcard of Paris is about as unlike the city as can be. To suppose that the distinction between pictorial or 'iconic' and other symbols rests on resemblance is nevertheless a prevalent and pernicious mistake. In the preceding chapter we saw in some detail why competence to understand a new picture cannot depend upon discerning its resemblance to what it represents. Here the further point is that such resemblance cannot even account for the difference between symbols that depict and those that do not.

But among symbols that depict, aren't those the more realistic that more closely resemble what they depict? This too is askew insofar as it suggests that comparative likeness is an antecedent constant that stands as the measure of realism. Likeness is not, for example, a matter of how many properties two things have in common; for every two things have exactly the same number of properties in common. Likeness varies with the comparative importance among the common properties and thus with interest, context, and custom. In a given phase of a given culture, a picture counts as realistic, in one common usage,[2] to the extent that it depicts in the accustomed way; realism is consonance with current pictorial practice. By giving prominence to certain features that such pictures share with their subjects, that practice contributes to *making* these pictures more like their subjects—and even affects what constitutes resemblance between objects. Both the realism and the likeness may increase or diminish or vanish entirely with a change in custom. Degrees of resemblance and of realism are transient interacting properties that fluctuate with practice.

Still, though thus intricately related to realism, resemblance does not distinguish, among symbols, between pictures and non-

2. On the various uses of "realistic", see "Three Types of Realism", in *MM*, pp. 126–130.

pictures. Words that become hackneyed and haggard do not turn into pictures. What, then, does distinguish pictorial representation from, say, verbal description?

Nowhere in my writing to date have I proposed a definition of depiction, but have only suggested that the everyday classification of symbols into pictures and nonpictures is related in an important way to the line between symbols in a dense or 'analog' system and those in a finitely differentiated or 'digital' system. Being analog seems perhaps a necessary condition for a depiction, but not a sufficient one; an ungraduated thermometer indicates temperatures in an analog system but does not, in common parlance, picture them.

To come closer to defining depiction, we might exclude such cases as diagrams and ungraduated instruments by requiring in addition what I have called repleteness. A symbol is the more replete according as proportionately more of its features are functioning symbolically. For instance, in a linear diagram, only differences in position between points on the line, with respect to the coordinates, are significant; the thickness and color of the line do not matter. But in a line drawing—a linear depiction—all these and other features are significant. The drawing is more replete than the diagram, even if the same line functions on some occasions as drawing and on others as diagram. Depictions tend to be highly replete.

Repleteness, elsewhere in my work (*LA*, 252) listed as a symptom of the aesthetic, may thus also be a factor in depiction. Adding the requirement of comparative repleteness to that of being analog draws the line more tightly around the subclass of symbols that are depictions. Whether tightly enough calls for further examination, but before that we must consider more carefully whether our first condition may have already drawn the line too tightly in some places.

Is a depiction indeed always an analog symbol? Is density really a necessary condition for depiction? What looks like a clear counterexample is a portrait of Abraham Lincoln or of a unicorn made by filling in with black certain squares on a white grid (*MM*, 86 and note 20). Haven't we here a digital picture? And isn't the idea of defining the pictorial in terms of the analog thus thoroughly discredited?

We need to watch our language here. When proposed answers to a question turn out so wrong, the time has come to re-examine the terms of our discourse, the commonplace as well as the technical notions we are working with, and perhaps even the question we are trying to answer.

2. Notions

In the present section I want to review briefly, and to some extent revise, the basic vocabulary of the theory of symbols outlined in my earlier writing. The basic notion is *reference* or symbolization, the relation between a symbol and whatever it stands for in any way. As primitive, this relation is not defined but explicated in terms of its several varieties, among them (1) *denotation*, reference by a word or other label to something it applies to, as in naming or predication, and (2) *exemplification*, reference by an instance, as a sample, to a label denoting it. "Label" is to be read quite generally to include pictures as well as words; and in many contexts "label for" can be read alternatively as "property of". Reference may also be mediate, via a chain of links, each of them a case of denotation or exemplification. And reference may be literal or metaphorical; for example, "loud" denotes a given necktie metaphorically if at all, and a drawing exemplifies motion metaphorically if at all. *Expression* involves such metaphorical exemplification.

A symbol *scheme* is made up of *characters*, each of them a class of one or more individual symbols that are interchangeable— equivalent or character-indifferent—under that scheme. The written alphabet, for example, is a symbol scheme such that each letter consists of its many individual marks or inscriptions. In other schemes the characters may be individuals. "Symbol" applies equally to individual symbols and to characters consisting of several of them.

In all schemes we need consider, the several characters are disjoint; no two have any instances in common. Otherwise, in a string of replacements of one instance of a character by another, the beginning and the end may not be instances of the same character. In artificial schemes disjointness may be established by precept. In traditional schemes like the alphabet, disjointness may be established by practice, which refuses to accept any mark as, for example, both an "a" and a "d".

The characters of a scheme, even though disjoint, may or may not be *effectively differentiated*. Two characters K and K' are effectively differentiated if and only if for every mark m that does not belong to both, we can determine either that m does not belong to K or that m does not belong to K'. For example, suppose a character C_1 consists of line segments one-half inch long while C_2 consists of line segments one inch long. Every line segment is then readily determined either not to belong to C_1 or not to belong to C_2. But now suppose that C_3 consists of all line segments longer than one inch (or alternatively of line segments longer than one inch by some immeasurable fraction of an inch). Then there will be some line segment s so little longer than one inch that we cannot determine either that it is or is not longer than one inch and so cannot determine either that it does not belong to C_2 or that it does not belong to C_3. In this case differentiation is precluded by the specification of the characters. In practice what matters is not merely whether differentiation is theoretically possible but whether it can be accomplished by means available and appropriate to the given use of the given scheme. Such effective differentiation obviously varies with circumstances. In some cases, highly precise measurements may be called for; in others, mere matching counts as lack of differentiation. Furthermore, differentiation is not always in terms of measurement or judgments of matching and nonmatching but may involve, for example, considerations of context: two marks exactly the same in shape, size, color, and so on may be such that one is determined not to be an "a", the other determined not to be a "d", by taking into account surrounding letter-marks (*LA,* 137–140). In traditional schemes like the alphabet, differentiation as well as disjointness may be effected by a practice that excludes not only any mark belonging to two characters but any mark not determined not to belong to one or not to belong to the other of some two characters.

Differentiation as here construed is not a familiar notion, but the differentiated is enough akin to the digital that a scheme differentiated throughout—that is, such that every two of its characters are effectively differentiated—may be called *digital.* Nondigital schemes range from those with only two nondifferentiated characters through dense schemes in one or more dimensions; but the many varieties within this range need not much concern us here. We may merely distinguish as *analog* (with warnings against misleading suggestions of the term) schemes such that between each two characters there is in the scheme a path of pairs of nondifferentiated characters; that is, such that each two characters are related by the ancestral of nondifferentiation in the scheme.

Specification of a symbol scheme is purely syntactical, in terms of its characters without regard to whatever they stand for if anything. When a symbol scheme is considered together with whatever its characters refer to we speak of a *symbol system;* and obviously one scheme may be common to many different systems. Semantic features, such as the presence or absence of ambiguity, of semantic disjointness, and of semantic differentiation, become relevant when systems are in question. But for the present we may confine our attention to schemes.

3. Digital and Analog

Little of this was needed, of course, to make quite clear the fault of the dotted picture of Abraham Lincoln or a unicorn as a counterexample to the hypothesis that pictures must be analog symbols. But what disqualifies the counterexample also disqualifies the hypothesis itself. Isn't the dotted picture a digital picture? No, because—as our preliminary discussion did not carefully observe—no symbol by itself is digital, and none by itself is analog. "Digital" and "analog" apply not to symbols in isolation but to symbol schemes. Thus, since schemes are not pictures, and pictures are not schemes, the question just how the pictorial and the analog are related may give us some trouble.

Is the hypothesis under examination, then, that a picture must be a symbol in an analog scheme? And is the dotted picture thus a decisive counterexample? This formulation is hardly any better. For while the dotted picture belongs to a digital scheme, it also belongs, like every other symbol, to many an analog scheme; and indeed every picture, dotted or not, belongs to some digital schemes. As I shall illustrate below, symbols in general belong to schemes of both types and so do not sort into digital or analog according to the type of scheme they belong to. Hypothesis and counterexample again fail together.

Our dotted Abraham Lincoln (or unicorn) picture is a card with a pattern of black and white squares. It belongs to a scheme having as characters cards with squares with the same grid filled with black and white in different ways. For simplicity we may suppose the scheme to provide for[3] one and only one card for each different pattern. Among the cards of this pack, *A*, are some pictures, some inscriptions of letters, words, numerals, and so on, and some that are of no familiar category. The cards being effectively differentiated, the scheme is digital.

Now suppose we supplement *A* by providing for many more cards of the same size, one for each pattern filling the square with black, grays, white in any way, with no restriction to any grid, so that not only will all dotted patterns but all those with shadings of any kind be included. In this augmented pack, *A'*,

---

3. "Scheme" may refer to a set of characters or to a specification of such a set. Since exactly what characters actually exist over time is often indeterminable, what characters a specification provides for usually matters more.

every card is undifferentiated from many others; the scheme is analog, and even dense throughout. Yet A', though analog, includes A and many other digital schemes. Such digital sub-schemes may be thought of as resulting from an operation of *excision* upon A' that in one way or another removes at least enough characters to leave the remaining characters differentiated. For example, A results from removing characters from A' in any path of nondifferentiation steps between any two of the dotted characters of A. Yet a digital scheme need not consist of dotted characters, but may be made up of several shaded pictures. So long as they are effectively differentiated, and characters making up any connecting paths are excluded, the scheme is digital. In other words, nondotted pictures belong to as many digital schemes as do dotted pictures. In general, an analog scheme includes many digital schemes, and a digital scheme is included in many analog schemes; but obviously no digital scheme includes any analog scheme.

Pictures in A make up a digital scheme, pictures in A' an analog scheme. Again, letter marks in A make up a digital scheme, letter marks in A' an analog one. But in neither A nor A' do all different letter marks count as different characters. For instance, some marks in script, in Roman type, in Gothic calligraphy, and so on, all count as the same character, the same letter. Thus the letter scheme L in A' cannot be reached only by an excision that leaves undifferentiated islands of marks (islands such that every mark in one is effectively differentiated from every mark in every other) and has to be accompanied by an *equation*—that is, by counting all the marks in each island as character-indifferent, as equivalent and interchangeable under the scheme. In other words, while all marks in L are marks in A', still L and A' have no characters in common. Although the letter marks in A' make up an analog scheme, L is a digital scheme. But rather surprisingly perhaps, each character in L is an analog set of marks; the digital letter scheme consists of characters that are themselves internally non-digital.

4. Questions

All this discussion of digital and analog schemes and their interrelation hardly seems to help in defining the difference between pictures and other symbols. Pictures and nonpictures alike, dotted or not, belong to many digital and analog schemes. And how are pictures distinguished from the other symbols *within* a scheme? In *A* and in *A'*, for instance, some of the cards are pictures, some are not. What makes or marks the difference?

Persistent trouble in answering a question suggests looking hard at just what the question is. Not much review is needed to realize that discussions of this type here and elsewhere have often vacillated among and confused several different questions. We have asked at various times how to define depiction, how to distinguish pictures from all other symbols, how to distinguish the pictorial from the descriptive, and so on. Such questions differ from each other in important ways. Let us begin with one and work from there.

At times we have taken the task to be the formulation of necessary and sufficient conditions that will define depicting symbols in contradistinction to all others. But that needs refinement in some ways. In the first place, the task is not to distinguish symbols that depict from those that do not denote at all but rather to distinguish depictions, whether they denote anything or not, from other symbols; that is, to distinguish pictures, whether or not of actual subjects, from nonpictures. Second, our initial concern is with distinguishing pictures not in one fell swoop from *all* other symbols but specifically from names and descriptions—with distinguishing the pictorial from the linguistic or verbal.

5. Pictures and Predicates

We have seen abundantly that pictorial symbols cannot be distinguished by resembling what they denote, by being analog, or by belonging to analog schemes; for some pictures denote nothing, no symbol is analog or digital by itself, and all symbols belong to many digital and analog schemes. Furthermore, some schemes consisting entirely of pictures (for instance, the pictures in our pack *A* above) are digital.

But now consider two comprehensive schemes: *S*, consisting of all descriptions or *predicates* (including names, descriptive phrases, and so on) in a language such as English; and *S'*, consisting of all pictures (whatever, according to a given standard usage, is a picture or other pictorial symbol). That is, compare the presystematic notions of description and picture in a given culture. Now suppose that we are told of *S* and *S'* not which is the pictorial or which the verbal scheme but only the structures of the schemes, the relations of the characters in each to one another in terms of effective differentiation. How can we determine which is the pictorial scheme? Obviously any among the many differences between the two will suffice, but we want more than an *ad hoc* difference between *S* and *S'*, we want a difference that will serve generally to distinguish the full pictorial scheme from the full descriptive scheme of any language. The notable such difference is that *S'*, unlike *S*, is analog.[4] The pictorial and the analog are thus clearly related. A full scheme is pictorial *only if* analog, verbal *only if* digital. But it is *not* the case that a full scheme is pictorial *if* analog, verbal *if* digital. In other words, not every analog full scheme is pictorial and not every digital full scheme is verbal.

Thus we have not arrived at a definition of pictures, or pictorial schemes, or even of full pictorial schemes. We have distinguished the pictorial from the verbal among full schemes, but we have not distinguished the pictorial from other analog full schemes,

---

4. This does not apply generally to subschemes since a scheme consisting entirely of pictures (for example, those from our pack *A* above) may be digital. In a digital scheme a picture may serve as a letter or word. A symbol functions as a picture only when taken as a character in the full pictorial scheme. This has sometimes been overlooked to the detriment of experimentation on the difference between verbal and pictorial symbol processing.

nor the verbal from other digital full schemes. Making such further distinctions as wanted is legitimate step-by-step work in the theory of symbols. As suggested earlier, repleteness may enter into distinguishing the pictorial from the diagrammatic; and features distinguishing the notational from the verbal have been investigated in *Languages of Art* in some detail. But such work will not be carried further here; the primary undertaking of the present study is completed with drawing the major distinction between the pictorial and the verbal—between pictures and predicates.

That distinction has been drawn in terms of purely syntactical features, quite independently of what the symbols denote or otherwise refer to. That was of course inevitable since pictures include not only symbols such as unicorn pictures that only ostensibly denote but also abstract paintings, drawings, prints that do not even purport to denote but refer in other ways, as by exemplification and expression. What distinguishes pictorial symbols lies not in resemblance or any other relationship to anything they may refer to, but in their syntactical relationships to each other. The pictorial is distinguished not by the likeness of pictures to something else but by some lack of effective differentiation among them. Can it be that—ironically, iconically—a ghost of likeness, as nondifferentiation, sneaks back to haunt our distinction between pictures and predicates?

(*Goodman*)

PART THREE

PREMONITIONS

IX

The Epistemic Efficacy of Stupidity

1. Embarrassments of Intelligence

Socrates maintained that he was the wisest of men in that he alone knew that he knew nothing. Although his avowal is typically taken to be ironic, he may have been telling the truth. For currently popular theories of knowledge have the surprising consequence that stupidity can enhance, and intelligence diminish, one's prospects for knowledge. So if any of these theories is correct, Socrates may have known less than others precisely because he was wiser than they.

I will show that an unwitting bias in favor of stupidity is characteristic of both internalist and externalist theories of knowledge. It derives from the shared convictions that (a) our epistemic goal is to accept (or believe) a sentence if it is true and reject (or

I am grateful to Warren Goldfarb for sharing his knowledge of wines with me, and to Kenneth Winkler for sharing his knowledge of birds.

disbelieve) it if it is false, and (b) the standard for acceptability cannot be set too high, else skepticism will prevail. The epistemic inutility of intelligence that follows is not the skeptic's fatalistic conclusion that since no one knows anything, dullards are no worse off than the rest. It is the more disconcerting result that since qualities of mind such as sensitivity, breadth, and logical acumen often interfere with the satisfaction of the requirements for knowledge, individuals deficient in such qualities have an epistemic edge. The quest for knowledge may then be furthered by the cultivation of obtuseness.

It would be tedious to demonstrate that this follows from all current theories of knowledge. So I have chosen to focus on four— two externalist and two internalist. They represent dominant strains in contemporary epistemological theorizing. And the difficulties I find are not difficulties in detail. So if all four find cognitive deficiencies conducive to knowledge, there will be reason to suspect that a commitment to the epistemic efficacy of stupidity is endemic to current epistemology. Toward the end of this chapter I consider what to make of this finding.

Contemporary epistemologists agree on this much at least: however good one's grounds for p, still, if p is false, one cannot know that p; knowledge then requires truth. Moreover, one cannot know that p without being cognitively committed to p; knowledge also requires belief or acceptance. And one cannot know that p if one's true belief that p is accidental; so knowledge requires a tether.

Internalists take the tether to be epistemic. Knowledge, they maintain, is tied down by justification that is epistemically accessible to the knowing subject. Disagreements among them concern the criteria for epistemic accessibility and the range of accessible information the subject need take into account. So they differ over the epistemic status of, for instance, unacknowledged implications of things one explicitly knows, or of undermining evidence one does not, but could, possess.

Externalists take the tether to be metaphysical. For a true belief to amount to knowledge, they contend, it must be necessarily connected to the fact that makes it true, or to facts from which its truth follows. They differ over the type of necessity required, but agree that it need not be within the subject's ken. An individual can know that p even if he is unaware that his belief that p is appropriately related to the facts. Some take the metaphysical tether, known or unknown, to constitute the justification for a belief, thereby conceding that justification may be epistemically inaccessible. Others follow internalism in requiring justification to be epistemically accessible, but deny that justification is integral to or necessary for knowledge. To avoid confusion, I will speak of external tethers, leaving it open whether a belief's tether provides its justification.

2. Knowledge from Outside

Causal theories of knowledge maintain that for a subject to know that p, his true belief that p must be caused by the fact that p or by facts from which it follows that p.[1] Sophisticated versions require that the causal connection be lawlike, so that knowledge cannot result from a fortuitous commingling of circumstances. Such theories account for inferential knowledge by claiming that inferential and logical relations may be parts of causal chains.

According to a causal theory then, my true belief that there is a yellow surface before me is caused by a neurophysiological response to the presence of yellow in my visual field. A sequence of optical and neural events linking the surface with a brain state is responsible for the production of my belief. If that sequence instantiates a natural law, I know that the surface is yellow. It is no accident that I believe what I do; for, given the laws of nature

---

1. Alvin Goldman, "A Causal Theory of Knowing", *Journal of Philosophy* 64 (1967) 357–372; and "Discrimination and Perceptual Knowledge", *Journal of Philosophy* 73 (1976) 771–791.

and the circumstances in which I find myself, my belief is a necessary consequence of the fact that the surface is yellow.

Such causal connections are common. It is no accident that normal perceivers typically believe objects to be the colors those objects actually are; for their beliefs are normally caused by the law-governed response of the human nervous system to the presence of those colors. That being so, causal theorists contend, normal perceivers generally know the colors of the objects they perceive. Since causal theories do not require epistemically accessible justification, they can recognize that unreflective and unintelligent people are often in a position to know. Watson is as capable as Holmes of knowing that the surface before him is yellow. And this is as it should be. Cognitive virtuosity is hardly required for knowledge of this kind.

But seemingly parallel conclusions are less comfortable. Consider one involving the sense of taste. Holmes, we may suppose, is an oenophile, while Watson is oblivious to all but the most obvious differences among wines. The two share a bottle of Bordeaux, and because it stimulates the appropriate nerve endings and brings about the proper neurological connections, it causes each to believe that he is drinking Bordeaux. (For vividness we can assume that their reactions do not differ neurologically.) According to causal theories, both Holmes and Watson know that the wine they are drinking is Bordeaux. The fact that Watson cannot tell a Bordeaux from a muscatel does not prevent him from knowing about this wine, for it does not intrude upon the causal chain leading to his current belief. And unless we are prepared to conclude that Holmes lacks knowledge, we cannot dismiss the chain of neurological events as anomalous. If a causal law is instantiated in the production of Holmes's belief, it is instantiated in the production of Watson's; for their neurological reactions do not differ. If Holmes knows what he's drinking, so does Watson.

It follows from causal theories that subjects can 'luck into' knowledge. Given Watson's insensitivity to distinctions among wines, it is accidental that the lawful causal chain eventuates in a true belief. Despite its impeccable breeding, Watson's belief is unreliable.

The conviction that unreliability precludes knowledge leads some externalists to reliabilism—the view that knowledge depends on a belief's relation to truth in counterfactual as well as in actual circumstances. On a reliabilist account, a properly tethered belief is, roughly, one the subject would harbor if it were true and would not harbor, at least on account of that tether, if it were false.[2] The truth of a properly tethered belief is no accident; for such a belief tracks truth across possible worlds.

Reliabilism concludes—correctly, it seems—that Watson does not know; for he would believe he was drinking Bordeaux even if he were drinking muscatel. The problem is that Holmes apparently fares no better. Although he can tell Bordeaux from muscatel, he cannot infallibly discriminate Bordeaux from all other sources of sensory stimulation. So Holmes, like Watson, fails the subjunctive test; there are non-Bordeaux he would believe to be Bordeaux, and Bordeaux he would believe to be non-Bordeaux.

Indeed, a full-blooded subjunctive requirement seems practically impossible to satisfy. So reliabilists moderate their demands by restricting the scope of the counterfactual condition to relevant alternatives. Holmes's belief needn't track truth through the minefields set out by malevolent demons in order to qualify as knowledge.

His epistemic prospects clearly depend on what alternatives count as relevant. If knowledge is to be possible at all, the skeptic's bogies—the machinations of malevolent demons and manipulative neurosurgeons—must be excluded as irrelevant. If all other actual wines are relevant alternatives for Holmes, then in order to know, he needs the ability to discriminate between Bordeaux

2. Robert Nozick, *Philosophical Explanations* (Cambridge, Mass.: Harvard University Press, 1981), pp. 172–196; and Fred Dretske, "Conclusive Reasons", *Australasian Journal of Philosophy* 49 (1971) 1–22.

and every other wine. The obstacles to knowledge then remain formidable. But the class of relevant alternatives might be narrower still. Perhaps it is limited to wines Holmes is likely to encounter, or even to the wines in his own cellar. Then his powers of discrimination need not be so great. If he can distinguish Bordeaux from the other members of fairly restricted classes of wines, he is in a position to know what he's drinking.

Reliabilist requirements for knowledge are variable, expanding and contracting with the range of relevant alternatives. Against the background of one set of alternatives, Holmes knows; against the background of another, he does not. Indeed, if the range is sufficiently restricted or gerrymandered, even Watson turns out to know; for the possibility that the wine is muscatel can be excluded as irrelevant. Apparently any true belief can be constituted as knowledge by suitably configuring the range of relevant alternatives. The epistemic status of a true belief thus depends on the selection of such a range; and without criteria to guide us, it is hard to avoid the appearance of begging the question in making a selection. Still, Holmes's epistemic situation is better than Watson's in that significantly more austere restrictions are required to constitute Watson's belief as knowledge. In this respect at least, the smarter man has an epistemic advantage.

It is not clear, though, that Holmes can sustain his advantage. Watson, we may suppose, reliably classifies wines as *rotgut, table wine,* and what he calls *'vintage stuff'*; and his beliefs about wine quality result from lawlike causal chains. So according to both reliabilist and causal theories, Watson knows he's drinking rotgut.

Holmes knows nothing of the sort. 'Rotgut' is not part of his conceptual repertoire, so he formulates no beliefs about rotgut. Since belief is required for knowledge, Watson knows something about their shared experience that Holmes does not. Still, Holmes brings to the wine tasting a wealth of refined, delicate distinctions. The first sip convinces him that he's drinking a 1986 Thunderbird, made from a resoundingly inferior grape grown in vacant lots just off the Santa Monica Freeway; a wine aged for a week in a plastic vat previously used to launder sweat socks. Holmes, with his more sensitive perceptual and conceptual categories, seems to be in a position to know a good deal more than Watson. Being able to frame more hypotheses, he has more candidates for knowledge than Watson does.

The problem is this: the more distinctions a system of categories admits, the less difference there is between adjacent categories. As we refine our conceptual schemes, we increase our chances of error. Although Holmes can usually tell the vintage of the wine he's drinking, no more than anyone else is he infallible. The perceptible differences among vintages are often extremely subtle and difficult to discern. Common conditions—the beginnings of a head cold, a poorly rinsed glass, a moment's inattentiveness, a stuffy room—can throw the most sensitive palate off, leading the taster to confuse a Margaux with a St. Julien. So Holmes's true belief that he's drinking a Margaux does not track truth very far. Were he victim to such contingencies, he would think he was drinking one wine when he was drinking another. The sources of error here are not hyperbolic constructions or remote possibilities, but everyday eventualities. So they cannot legitimately be excluded by circumscribing the range of relevant alternatives. On a reliabilist theory, Holmes does not know; nor does anyone else whose judgments are vulnerable to such contingencies. The more delicate our distinctions, the more easily circumstances conspire to confound judgment. So as we refine our categories, we diminish our prospects for knowledge.

Causal theories seem to do better here, being indifferent to the counterfactuals that confute the reliabilist. If Holmes's belief that he is drinking a Margaux is caused by the fact that he's drinking a Margaux and if the causal chain that eventuates in that belief instantiates a law of nature, Holmes knows that he's drinking a Margaux. It seems then that the causal theory can accommodate increasing categorial refinement, being concerned solely with the genesis of actual beliefs; for there is no a priori limit to the precision of beliefs that can be lawfully generated.

The problem is that Holmes is no dummy. He is well aware of the circumstances that might mislead—of the availability of wines easily mistaken for a Margaux, and of the physiological and environmental conditions that can affect the palate. And he realizes that he cannot be confident that no such circumstances obtain. This gives him pause. Although he strongly suspects that he is imbibing a Margaux, he can't bring himself fully to believe it. And without belief there is no knowledge. So Holmes's appreciation of the precariousness of his epistemic situation prevents him from knowing.

Respect for evidence may also inhibit knowledge. Suppose there is such a thing as extrasensory perception, and that the absence of evidence for such a faculty is due to the fact that genuine extrasensory perceptions are extremely hard to distinguish from a variety of unreliable sources of intimation.[3] Watson and Holmes are equally extrasensorily perceptive. But Watson is credulous; Holmes is not. So Watson believes the deliverances of ESP, dismissing the evidence out of hand. Holmes respects the evidence and the methods of the sciences that produced it. So he does not credit his extrasensory perceptions. Although he cannot prevent himself from experiencing them, he withholds belief; for he can find no legitimate grounds for the suspicions they produce. Holmes then does not know; his epistemic scruples prevent him from forming the requisite beliefs.

On both causal and reliabilist accounts, Watson does know. Extrasensory perceptions yield true beliefs via lawful, if unrecognized, causal chains. And if ESP is reliable (even though we have no reason to think it is), Watson would believe its deliverances if they were true, and would not believe them via ESP if they were false. So Watson's obliviousness to the evidence serves him well; it enables him to know.

3. This example is a variant of one developed by Laurence Bonjour in "Externalist Theories of Empirical Knowledge", in *Midwest Studies in Philosophy V*, ed. Peter A. French, Theodore E. Uehling, Jr., and Howard K. Wettstein (Minneapolis: University of Minnesota Press, 1980), pp. 53–73.

In summary, externalism favors the employment of crude categories; for refinements invite error and unreliability. If our objective is to believe what is true and disbelieve what is false, it is reasonable to restrict opportunites for belief to cases in which truth and falsity are easily distinguished.

Externalism also favors obliviousness to evidence. A subject is affected by evidence if that evidence initiates the causal chain or activates the reliable mechanism responsible for his belief. But there is no epistemic advantage to his being aware of the evidence, for a belief's tether is not strengthened by the subject's cognizance of its constitution. Indeed, knowledge may be lost by his attempt to give evidence its due. For evidence can mislead, inhibiting the adoption of true, tethered beliefs and encouraging the adoption of false, untethered ones. We do best then to let evidence exercise its effect subliminally when it is integral to a belief's tether, and to ignore it when it is not.

Finally, externalism favors unreflectiveness about one's epistemic circumstances. Indeed, obliviousness to evidence is but a special case of this. Appreciation of the opportunities for error and of the claims of alternative hypotheses cause reservations, leading the reflective agent to suspend judgment. A heady, if unfounded, confidence, born of the ability to overlook obstacles, supplies the unreflective subject with a goodly store of beliefs, many of which turn out to be true and tethered. The unreflective subject succeeds or fails depending on the proportion of true, tethered beliefs in his doxastic system. But the reflective subject is bound to fail; for unless he is willing to believe, he is in no position to know. He neither believes what is true nor disbelieves what is false; lacking sufficient evidence, he suspends judgment.

3. Knowledge from Inside

Internalism maintains that a claim is justified to the extent that it is reasonable in light of what is already known. Justification thus depends on coherence with a system of already accepted claims.[4] Some take the relevant system to be individualist; others take it to be social. I shall consider accounts of both kinds.

Keith Lehrer's internalism is individualistic.[5] He holds that the justification for a hypothesis is a matter of its coherence with a system of claims the subject already accepts, where a statement coheres with a system if its acceptance is more reasonable relative to that system than is the acceptance of any competing claim. Epistemic justification does not, of course, demand coherence with everything the subject holds. He may accept statements for purposes other than knowledge; and coherence with such statements confers no epistemic status. If, for example, he accepts a religious doctrine on the basis of faith and for the purpose of salvation, the coherence of a claim with that doctrine would be epistemologically irrelevant. What is required for epistemic justification, Lehrer contends, is that a hypothesis cohere with the statements the subject accepts for the purpose of knowledge. These statements constitute his personal acceptance system; and he is personally justified in accepting anything that coheres with that system. But personal justification is not enough; for personal acceptance systems typically contain falsehoods. And a statement that coheres with antecedently accepted falsehoods is not on that account a viable candidate for knowledge. Candidacy is restricted to statements that also belong to the subject's verific acceptance system—the system that results when his personal acceptance system is purged of all error. A claim that coheres with both is, Lehrer believes, completely justified for the subject. For its jus-

4. Some internalists—such as Chisholm—recognize basic statements that are supposed to be inherently reasonable. But they acknowledge that most statements are not basic, so justification is mostly a matter of coherence. Cf. Roderick Chisholm, *The Foundations of Knowing* (Minneapolis: University of Minnesota Press, 1982). Moreover,' their admission of inherently reasonable statements is problematic. For it would not be reasonable on internalist grounds to accept a putatively basic statement that conflicted with the appropriate background system; I ought not accept the claim that I see something red if I am justifiably convinced that I am color blind.

5. Keith Lehrer, "The Coherence Theory of Knowledge", *Philosophical Topics* 14 (1986) 5–25.

tification does not depend essentially on any false belief; and relative to the truths the subject believes, it is more reasonable than any of its rivals. Indeed, on Lehrer's account, an accepted, completely justified truth is knowledge.

What coheres with a narrow system can fail to cohere with a broader one. So Watson, with his limited purview, knows things that Holmes, burdened with a more comprehensive one, does not. Upon sighting a bird, Holmes and Watson form the belief that it is a superb starling. Watson's relevant background beliefs are truths about the characteristic markings of superb starlings. He has no beliefs about the bird's habitat; for, although he studiously attends to the pictures in the bird watcher's manual, he ignores the accompanying text. Given the information in his acceptance system, Watson's belief is completely justified. And since the bird, an escapee from the London Zoo, is in fact a superb starling, Watson knows that it is. Holmes, however, does not. Although he too recognizes that the bird in question has the markings of a superb starling, he realizes that such birds, being indigenous to equatorial Africa, are unlikely to be found on Baker Street. So, relative to Holmes's acceptance system, it is at least as reasonable to suspect that they've sighted a strangely marked local bird. Watson's ignorance thus enables him to know what Holmes cannot. The fact that prevents Holmes from knowing, being external to Watson's acceptance system, cannot undermine Watson's justification.[6]

The point is not that Watson benefits from ignorance of one specific, and in this case misleading, fact. It is rather that relatively sparse systems may be better sources of knowledge than richer systems. Watson can appeal only to markings to determine what kind of bird he's looking at. Still, his resources are sufficient for complete justification and knowledge. Holmes's system includes information about markings and about habitat. So coherence with

6. Cf. Carl Ginet, "Knowing Less by Knowing More", in French, Uehling, and Wettstein, *Midwest Studies in Philosophy V*, pp. 151–162.

Holmes's system is harder to achieve. But its achievement gives Holmes no more than Watson already has—complete justification and (often) knowledge. When, as in the present case, beliefs about habitat undermine an identification based on markings, Holmes is not justified in accepting any identification. Watson may then know what the bird is; Holmes surely does not. So if an acceptance system is sufficient to generate knowledge about a subject, additional information about that subject is otiose and potentially detrimental. Its incorporation into the system increases the difficulty of achieving coherence, making it harder to know.

This suggests that Holmes could protect his justification and enhance his epistemic prospects by isolating his system from potential defeaters. So long as he remains ignorant of history, for example, his justification cannot be undermined by unfortunate historical precedents. Lehrer suggests, however, that such self-conscious protectionism would be incompatible with the quest for knowledge. "A person who seeks after truth in a disinterested and impartial manner would not arbitrarily restrict his beliefs in this way."[7] Such protectionism is not obviously arbitrary. Given the goal of knowledge, it seems a reasonable strategy to accept the minimum required to generate completely justified true beliefs. For, as Holmes's predicament shows, to include superfluous information is to ask for trouble. Still, if such intentional restrictions on the scope of his acceptance system are arbitrary, Holmes could not, Lehrer believes, adopt Watson's stance without foresaking the quest for knowledge.

But Watson comes by his limitations naturally. So his motives as a knowledge seeker cannot be impugned because of his failure to incorporate certain information into his acceptance system. Indeed, he may be incapable of doing so. Suppose Holmes's confounding belief derives from a complex statistical generalization correlating the intensity of a bird's coloration with the mean temperature of its habitat—a generalization from which it follows

7. Keith Lehrer, *Knowledge* (Oxford: Oxford University Press, 1974), p. 209.

that a brightly colored bird like the superb starling is unlikely to be found in a temperate climate. Watson does not know the generalization; moreover, he could not understand or appreciate its import, were it imparted to him. So neither it nor its denial can enter into his personal acceptance system. As a result, the generalization cannot defeat any of his completely justified beliefs. For epistemically inaccessible truths are, for the internalist, epistemically inert. It is then his stupidity, not just his ignorance, that enables Watson to know what the more intelligent Holmes cannot.

Like externalism, individualist internalism favors the employment of crude categories, where differences are stark and instantiation is easily verified. Reasonably conscientious application of such a system typically produces knowledge. But when category systems admit of subtle distinctions, knowledge is much harder to achieve. It is fairly easy to tell whether something is a bird; fairly hard to tell whether it is a tree pipit. So since Watson is given to entertaining hypotheses at the level of

x is a bird

he's likely to generate a good deal of (trivial) knowledge. Since Holmes draws finer distinctions, he has a harder time. Often no single classification at the species level, for example, is most reasonable; so none coheres with his personal acceptance system. Moreover, if one alternative does prevail, it is apt not to beat its competition by much. So the least inaccuracy in his relevant background beliefs may exclude it from his verific acceptance system.

If the only discernible difference Holmes recognizes between a tree pipit and a buff meadow pipit is that the former is slightly plumper than the latter, his justification is defeated if he's even slightly wrong about how plump a tree pipit is expected to be. So Watson is likely to come away from a bird-watching expedition with a lot more knowledge than Holmes. For Watson will have formed many completely justified beliefs

x_1 is a bird

x_2 is a bird

. . .

x_n is a bird.

Holmes, having attempted more precise classifications of $x_1, \ldots,$ x_n, will have encountered some birds he could not identify, some whose identification he was not personally justified in accepting, some whose identification he was not completely justified in accepting, and some in which the identification he was completely justified in accepting was nonetheless false. Indeed, under the circumstances, Holmes might reasonably refrain from accepting any claims at this level of refinement. Since he desires to disbelieve falsehoods as well as to believe truths, he would be wise to suspend judgment where the prospect of error looms large. Here again, it seems rational to revert to Watson's safer stance. For Watson achieves the goal of believing truths and disbelieving falsehoods far better than Holmes does.

This might be doubted. It might seem that Holmes, having a richer cognitive repertoire, is in a position to form more undefeated justified true beliefs than Watson. If so, he knows more than Watson, even though Watson knows some things he does not. But the premiss is false; for Watson can generate undefeated justified true beliefs at least as quickly as Holmes. Of course, Watson's will tend to be trivial, banal, and boring, while Holmes's are often original, interesting, and important. But contemporary epistemology does not have the resources to discriminate between significant and insignificant beliefs. So it has no basis for ruling that Holmes's justified true beliefs are epistemically better than Watson's.

We are reluctant to credit Watson with knowledge because he neglects information that seems plainly relevant to the justifiability of his beliefs. But we can't fault him merely for ignoring information that bears on the topic of his concern; such information is inexhaustible, so some of it is bound to be ignored. If we consider Holmes's beliefs justified, it is because we think he has taken enough into account. He has neglected no important information and no significant inference.

But if taking enough into account isn't taking everything into account, and isn't taking into account only what the subject considers relevant, how is it determined? Gilbert Harman suggests that 'enough' here is a social matter—that the standards of the epistemic community decide what information is important, what inferences are significant, how much is required in order to know.[8] Since knowledge is an ordinary, not an extraordinary, cognitive achievement, the standards in question must be ones that normal members of the community normally meet. Watson's justification is inadequate then when it omits reasons that normal members of the community would normally invoke to justify such a belief.

The socialization of justification has two consequences worth noting. First, justifiedness varies with community standards. Holmes's belief may be justified according to the standards of one epistemic community and fail to be justified according to those of another. And variability in the requirements on justification results in variability in knowledge.[9] Holmes knows relative to one set of standards, but does not know relative to another. Moreover, relative to a community with sufficiently lax or peculiar standards, Watson too has justification and knowledge.

Second, epistemic accessibility is construed socially. Epistemic resources count as accessible if they are available to normal members of the community, even if the peculiarities of an individual's situation make them unavailable to him. It follows that information the subject does not possess and inferences he does not draw can defeat his justification if that information is known to, or those inferences drawn by, normal members of the community. The widely known fact that London is inhospitable to tropical birds can defeat Watson's justification, even though he is unaware

8. Gilbert Harman, *Thought* (Princeton: Princeton University Press, 1973), pp. 142–154.

9. Stewart Cohen, "Knowledge and Context", *Journal of Philosophy* 83 (1986) 579.

of that fact. And the easy inference from the extreme improbability of encountering a tropical bird on Baker Street to the unreasonableness of believing one has done so can defeat his justification, even though he fails to draw that inference.

Since Holmes more than satisfies community standards, his epistemic success may seem assured. But it is not; for by excelling, he invites trouble.

Being an acute reasoner, Holmes validly infers that recent fluctuations in grain prices discredit the claim that the prime minister lied about the prospects for peace. Normal members of the community lack the acumen to recognize the relevance of grain prices to the prime minister's statement, and to draw the proper inference from them. So the considerations Holmes adduces are too arcane to undermine the social justification for the claim. As it turns out, the prime minister did lie; the economic indicators are misleading. Since normal members of the community are not bound to consider those indicators, their justification is intact. So they know that the prime minister lied. What about Holmes? If he need only satisfy the community's standards, "The prime minister lied" is justified for him, since he is privy to all the information that justifies normal members of the community in their belief. But he pays for his justification by sacrificing his belief. Realizing that the evidence of the grain prices discredits the community's justification, he cannot consider himself justified in believing the prime minister lied. So, being rational, he does not believe it. And without belief, there is no knowledge.

Because he is smarter than others, Holmes is willy-nilly answerable to more exacting standards. He cannot ignore truths within his ken merely because others are incapable of appreciating their significance. Holmes thus fails to know, although his intellectual inferiors succeed.

Again, if Holmes's categories are more refined than those employed by the community at large, his judgments cannot be sustained by community standards. But without socially shared standards for their justification, those judgments are not candidates for knowledge. Holmes's additional conceptual and perceptual sensitivity does not then enable him to know what normal members of the community cannot. Indeed, the social requirements on justification are such that it is impossible for someone to know what normal members of the community cannot.

Since social internalism takes knowledge to be relative to an epistemic community, it might seem to have the resources to block these untoward results. Can't we give Holmes his due by evaluating his beliefs in terms of the standards of a more intelligent, sensitive community? The difficulty is that *any* epistemic community will have members whose cognitive abilities exceed the norm. So Holmes's predicament will recur no matter how we adjust the membership conditions on the relevant epistemic community.

Internalism, whether individual or social, thus favors conformity and a sort of cognitive minimalism. A person's epistemic prospects are best if his doxastic system includes no more than is necessary to justify his beliefs. Additional information and greater abilities produce no epistemic advantage; and they have the capacity to undermine the justification the minimal system supplies.

4. Knowledge Aside

It should now be obvious that Holmes's predicament is endemic to contemporary epistemology. And this is no surprise. For it results from features that proponents count as virtues of their theories—features that yield the ability to make do, in one way or another, with less than ideal justification. The very limitations on the requirements for knowledge which make it possible for the Watsons of the world to know make knowledge more difficult for individuals like Holmes.

This conclusion should not be construed as a counterexample to currently popular theories. In some cases at least, it seems reasonable to believe that Watson knows more than Holmes. The blunt man of solid, uninspired common sense, being untroubled by subtleties, may know what's what, while the more sensitive, finely tuned intelligence is distracted by nuances. Nor is it likely that a further condition on knowledge could redress the balance in favor of intelligence. For to attempt to redress that balance would be to move again in the direction of ideal justification, back into the snares of the skeptic.

What Holmes's predicament shows, I believe, is that knowledge, as contemporary theories conceive it, is not and ought not be our overriding cognitive objective. For to treat it as such is to devalue cognitive excellences such as conceptual and perceptual sensitivity, logical acumen, breadth and depth of understanding, and the capacity to distinguish important from trivial truths. Even when Watson knows more than Holmes, he does not appear to be cognitively better off.

This suggests that it is unwise to restrict epistemology to the study of what contemporary theories count as knowledge. What is wanted is a wide-ranging study of cognitive excellences of all sorts, and of the ways they contribute to or interfere with one another's realization. The fruits of such a study might enable us to understand how Socrates, knowing nothing, could be the wisest of men.

(*Elgin*)

X

A Reconception
of Philosophy

1. Some Misconceptions

Philosophy is in trouble again—and again and again. What began in wonder ends in surrender. Our hypotheses, descriptions, depictions, perceptions cannot be checked against the inaccessible 'external world'. All hope of arriving at justified and certain truth vanishes. In the face of such manifest failure, some philosophers quit, some carry on a futile struggle, and some glory in the liberation of concluding that anything goes—even though then the statement "Nothing goes" also goes as does the statement "Some things don't go".

Recurrent disaster amounts to a *reductio ad absurdum* of philosophy as commonly conceived—of what are taken to be some central ideas and questions of philosophy. Defeat and confusion are built into the notions of truth and certainty and knowledge. Some revisions or replacements or supplements are called for, some overhauling of conceptual equipment, some reconception of philosophy.

The guilty standard concepts not only raise unanswerable questions but are, insofar as clear at all, constricted and obtuse. The primary aim of what we shall propose is not avoidance of trouble but rather development of wider-ranging and more sensitive instruments. That cannot be accomplished quickly, but will have to begin with suggestions, sketches, examples, that will need amplification, sharpening, trial, and amendment. First, let's consider what's wrong with some familiar central concepts.

The faults of *truth* are many and grave. Construed as correspondence between discourse and the readymade world beyond discourse, it runs into double trouble: there is no such world independent of description; and correspondence between description and the undescribed is incomprehensible. Truth is a useful classification of statements, but must be conceived in some other way.

Furthermore, truth is an excessively *narrow* notion. Its range is limited to the verbal and, within the verbal, to statements. It does not apply to predicates or clauses or to such sentences as questions or instructions. And it pertains only to what a statement *says*, taking no account of what it may refer to in other ways, as by exemplification or expression or allusion.

Finally, even within its own narrow province, truth is not the only and often not the overriding consideration. Truth matters little in a statement that is not to the point: "2 + 2 = 4" is no answer to the question "What color is snow?" And in science as well as in daily life, admittedly false approximations generally take precedence over truths and even over readily available closer approximations. Simple summaries and smooth curves become the facts and laws that we work and live by.

Thus truth needs help. *Certainty*, though, is beyond help. Proof is clearly neither a sufficient nor a necessary condition for certainty since certainty of unproved premisses is required for certainty of conclusion. Certainty tangles two widely disparate notions. Does certainty amount to fervent belief, utter conviction, fond faith? Then it attaches sometimes to true, sometimes to false, statements. Or does certainty amount to incontrovertibility? Then since all true statements are incontrovertible, all are certain. And incidentally, so are some false statements if there are statements that are neither demonstrably true nor demonstrably false. Certainty is a woefully uncertain notion.

Knowledge involves both truth and certainty, and suffers the ailments of both along with further complications. Certainty of truth that arises from fallacy or fealty or intoxication or hypnosis does not count as knowledge. Justification is needed; and such justification cannot consist of proof alone, for proof provides justification only if the premisses are also somehow justified. What justifies certainty is hard to say when we have no clear idea what certainty is. Alternative versions of knowledge sometimes replace certainty by some sort of probability or by belief just short of utter conviction. But suppose you justifiably believe that the top card on a given well-shuffled pack is not the two of diamonds, and suppose this turns out to be true. Can you claim to have known it? Knowledge as uncertain is hardly a happier notion than knowledge as certain. As Quine remarks, "Epistemology, or the theory of knowledge, blushes for its name."[1]

Here then are some samples of deficiencies in what are commonly taken as key concepts in philosophy—some potholes, some roadblocks, some cracks in the infrastructure. Let's explore some suggestions toward renovation.

2. Faults of Truth

For a concept with greater reach than truth, consider *rightness*. "Right" and "wrong" apply to symbols of all kinds, verbal and nonverbal. Not only statements but demands and queries, words, categories, pictures, diagrams, samples, designs, musical pas-

---

1. W. V. Quine, "Relativism and Absolutism", *The Monist* 67 (1984) 295.

sages and performances, and symbols of any other sort may be right or wrong. Moreover, rightness pertains to all the ways that symbols function. A symbol may be right or wrong in what it says, denotes, exemplifies, expresses, or refers to via a homogeneous or heterogeneous chain of referential steps; rightness, unlike truth, is multidimensional. And sometimes, as in the case of right mistakes, what is wrong in one way may be right in another. In ordinary use, indeed, "right" and "wrong" range *too* wide for our purposes since they apply also to nonsymbols and to nonreferential aspects of symbols. A tennis stroke may be right or wrong, as may a reward or punishment, an arrow's aim, a medicine; a car may be tuned right or run wrong. Although everything in a world is version-dependent, so that all rightness has something to do with symbols, we are particularly concerned here with rightness of symbolic functioning.

Rightness even among statements often diverges from truth. Although snow is white, the statement "Snow is white" may not be right. It is wrong, because irrelevant, as an answer to the question how dense granite is, while the statement "Granite weighs one pound per cubic foot" is wrong because false. Yet some false statements may be right in other ways and in some contexts. For instance, a false utterance of "You are improving" may be a right remark to a discouraged student or a depressed patient; here rightness has to do with the *effect* of what is said. In other cases, rightness may involve serviceability for a scientific or other purpose. Boyle's law, though perhaps not exactly true[2] for any given

2. To relax a law by explicitly allowing for enough deviation may save truth but does not obviate the need for other criteria, since every alternative allowing at least that deviation will also be true. The right choice may be the formulation with the least allowance that eliminates violations and yet meets some standard of smoothness or simplicity. Notice further that the reports on the particular instances will themselves seldom be exactly true.

Professor Michael Benedikt has kindly called our attention to Anselm's fascinating discussion of truth and rightness in "Concerning Truth", in *Three Philosophical Dialogues*, ed. and trans. Jasper Hopkins and Herbert Richardson, vol. 1 of Anselm of Canter-

instance, is often right when a detailed report on thousands of data may be wrong because as little suited to the work in hand as are five million pennies for paying off a $50,000 mortgage. Rightness is plainly more complicated than truth and also more volatile, varying with circumstances that in no way affect truth.

Thus on many a score the idea that truth is simply the species of rightness that pertains to statements goes by the board. What emerges in its place is the realization that truth is but one among the factors—along with such others as relevance, effect, and use-ability—that sometimes enter into the rightness of what is said. Truth is an occasional ingredient in rightness.

In order to compare rightness with truth, we have been focusing on rightness with respect to what statements say. But statements and other symbols, verbal or not, can be right or wrong on various counts with respect to other ways they may symbolize. A statement in a poem or a passage in a cello sonata may be right or wrong in rhythms exemplified or feelings expressed. Patterns shown forth in a Bartok concerto or a Mondrian painting may be right; feelings expressed by cute curlicues on a crematorium or by a ponderous theater for Gilbert and Sullivan could be wrong.

The comparative importance of different kinds of rightness varies. A scientific treatise seldom expresses feeling, and when one does grumble or gloat, that is of little concern. On the other hand, what *Gulliver's Travels* literally says matters far less than what it conveys by more devious routes.

The ways of judging what is right in a cosmology, in a concept for microphysics, in composition or color in a painting, tempo in an orchestral performance, style in a novel, design in a building, and so on and on, are widely varied and up to practitioners and theoreticians in each field. Also rightness differs not only among

---

bury's *Theological Treatises* (Cambridge, Mass.: Harvard Divinity School Library, 1965), pp. 4–42. Anselm touches on many topics, such as tense and indicator words, other than those that concern us here. He aims, as we do not, at eventual identification of rightness with truth.

different fields but, as we have seen, among different aspects of a single symbol. No philosophical pronouncement can provide a general criterion or rules for determining rightness. Nevertheless, the different applications and procedures all have something important in common. They are all concerned with effecting a positive-negative dichotomy or a grading on a preferential scale, and they share other highly abstract but important features. The question what constitutes rightness in general has to be taken as asking for some characterization or sketch, in terms of such features, of what the various kinds of rightness have in common, not for a touchstone that will determine rightness in every or indeed any case, nor even for a formal definition.

Illustrations already given suggest that rightness is a matter of fitting and working. Since rightness is not confined to those symbols that state or describe or depict, the fitting here is not a fitting *onto*—not a correspondence or matching or mirroring of independent Reality—but a fitting *into* a context or discourse or standing complex of other symbols. On the one hand, fitting is not sheer coherence. Other factors such as seniority also count; the fabric, the background, that which is being fitted into, has some degree of inertia, some claim to preservation, some tentative priority over what is being fitted into it. We shall have more to say about this later. On the other hand, fitting is neither passive nor one-way, but an active process of fitting together; the fit has to be *made*, and the making may involve minor or major adjustments in what is being fitted *into* or what is being fitted *in* or both.

The fitting is tested by the working, by the forwarding of work in hand or in prospect. What counts is not so much the working of what is fitted in as the working of the resultant whole. The work in question may be of any kind, though we are here primarily concerned with cognitive work: with achieving a firmer and more comprehensive grasp, removing anomalies, making significant discriminations and connections, gaining new insights. Thus while our talk of working may echo pragmatism, we are by no means trying to reduce rightness, as some pragmatists try to reduce truth, to practicality;[3] running a machine successfuly does not amount to understanding it in all ways. And although we said that working tests fitting, the two are more intimately related than that; for the working is also a kind of fitting—fitting into a going operation or process or endeavor. Moreover, even what constitutes fitting and working may undergo change, may itself have to be adjusted in order to fit and work.

3. The Conviction of Certainty

In proposing rightness for a major role in our reconception, we did not jettison truth altogether but kept it, somewhat modified, for a subordinate role. In contrast, *certainty*—a pretentious muddle of the psychological and the pseudological—is unsalvageable. Alternatives such as probability, belief, and assent, pertaining to statements only, are too narrow for our purposes and otherwise unsuitable. Acceptance might be widened to include some non-statements, but *adoption* has salient advantages. We can adopt habits, strategies, vocabularies, styles, as well as statements. And while acceptance seems often to require and be accomplished by specific but passive declaration, no such declaration is necessary or sufficient for adoption. Adoption is a matter of putting to work, of making or trying to make a fit. To adopt a symbol is to incorporate it into the apparatus in use, the fabric being woven, the work in progress. The term "adoption" may be used variously for such an *act*, for the *state* of having been adopted and not since dropped, or for *what* is adopted in such an act or is in such a state.

Adoption does *not* imply any degree of confidence; it may be

3. But some pragmatists denounce practicalism; for example, C.S. Peirce writes: "True science is distinctively the study of useless things. For the useful things will get studied without the aid of scientific men. To employ these rare minds on such work is like running a steam engine by burning diamonds." Quoted by Israel Scheffler in *Four Pragmatists* (London: Routledge and Kegan Paul, 1974), p. 84, from *The Collected Papers of Charles Sanders Peirce*, ed. C. Hartshorne and P. Weiss, 1, p. 76.

merely on noncommittal trial, may result from random choice among equally unappealing alternatives, may even be—as in indirect proof—for testing what is thought to be quite wrong. But whether an adoption carries positive or negative or nil expectation of success, the overall effort is toward achieving a relatively durable but flexible and productive network of adoptions.

While adoption does not claim rightness, it may participate in the generation of rightness; for as an adoption continues in effect, what is adopted earns an increasing claim to rightness. In some notable instances, a category or predicate or hypothesis gains precedence over others through entrenchment—a result of continued or repeated use: what makes "All emeralds are green" right and "All emeralds are grue" wrong when both fit all available cases equally well is habit or practice. Entrenchment does not derive from rightness; rather, conversely, entrenchment is what, along with further fitting and working, *makes for* rightness.

Still, how can this be consonant with our earlier characterization of rightness as a matter of fitting and working? In the first place, adoption begins the effort to make a fit and put to work; thus the fitting and the working depend upon adoption. Moreover the fitting, as we have said, is not a mere fitting together of elements having equal status but a fitting of each new element into an already adopted background or apparatus or structure. Making the fit may indeed call for altering the background, for dropping or revising venerable adoptions; but the background yields less readily than new proposals. This provides some constancy under reconstruction, and differentiates among versions that have equal status on grounds of coherence alone. The background, under whatever name, consists at any time and for any context of what has been and still is adopted at that time and in that context.

A much earlier study examined how cognition proceeds from elements that have varying degrees of 'initial credibility' (*PP*, 60–68). That term has its drawbacks. "Initial" is sometimes mistaken for "the very first", "original", or even "innate", when all that was meant was *at the start* of a particular cognitive undertaking. Also "credibility" is a complex and problematic notion amounting to "entitlement to belief". What we are concerned with, rather than initial credibility, is *current adoption*.

To point out the part that habit, tradition, long-term adoption play in rightness is not by any means to stress conservation over innovation. For not only does the established background undergo continual if normally gradual change through adjustment to new elements, but also some relative stability is a necessary precondition for novelty. Innovation, after all, is alteration of established practices or penchants or principles. And in seeking adoptions that will last for a while, a major consideration is to develop background instruments that will accommodate and advance new inquiry and ideas.

4. Knowledge Unknown

Finally, knowledge, plagued with certainty and uncertainty alike, gives way in our reconception to *understanding*. Whereas knowledge typically requires truth, belief, and substantiation, understanding requires none of these. Statements can be understood regardless of their truth and regardless of belief in them; and we can understand requests and queries and verbs and dances, though these are neither true nor false, neither believed nor disbelieved, and subject neither to demonstration nor refutation. Much as rightness is broader in scope than truth, and adoption broader in scope than certainty, understanding is broader in scope than knowledge.

"Understanding" is a versatile term for a skill, a process, an accomplishment. First, the understanding is what might be called the cognitive 'faculty' in an inclusive sense: the collection of abilities to inquire and invent, discriminate and discover, connect and clarify, order and organize, adopt, test, reject. Second, understanding is the *process* of using such skills for the cognitive making and remaking of a world, worlds, or a world of worlds. The process goes on and on, for understanding is always partial;

fitting symbols or ways of symbolizing in and making them work is a task as varied as are symbol systems, referential relationships, and situations and objectives. Advancement of the understanding consists in improvement of the relevant skills or in applying them to expand or refine what is understood. Third, understanding is *what* the cognitive process achieves, somewhat as knowledge in one sense consists of what is known, though what is understood is not always believed or established as true.

5. A Reconception

All we have been able to do here is sketch, in the scantiest way, some first steps in a proposed reconception, but we hope this may suggest the general character of the proposal. We say *a* reconception of philosophy, not *the* reconception; and not revolution either, for the concepts given new prominence are not themselves new even if somewhat remodeled. On the other hand, what we are proposing is no retreat, no mere watering down of the prevailing conception. We have not dropped truth in favor of confirmation, certainty in favor of probability, or knowledge in favor of opinion; and we have not resigned to an unrestrained relativism. Rightness, though it sometimes involves truth, is— even where statements alone are concerned—a more stringent requirement pertaining not only to declaration but to all other ways of referring and to symbols that do not declare or denote at all. Adoption and understanding likewise pertain to symbols and symbolizing of all kinds.

Nor, let us remind you, is the proposed reconception designed to combat skepticism. We heartily concur with the skeptical conclusion that transcendent truth as well as certainty and knowledge are unattainable. This conclusion results not from gross deficiencies in human cognitive capacity but from fatal flaws in the very notions of truth, certainty, and knowledge. Thus a reconception was called for that, while entirely compatible with the impossibility of arriving at (transcendent) truth or certainty or knowledge, has greater scope and other purposes.

All this radically alters the way of looking upon the cognitive endeavor.[4] Taken as the pursuit of *knowledge*, that endeavor starts from sure truths and seeks by means of derivation, observation, and experiment to discover others and so to arrive at an accurate and comprehensive description of 'the real' readymade world. The foundation is supposedly solid, the methods prescribed, the goal eternal transcendent truth. In contrast, taken as the advancement of *understanding*, the cognitive endeavor starts from what happens to be currently adopted and proceeds to integrate and organize, weed out and supplement, not in order to arrive at truth about something already made but in order to make something right—to construct something that works cognitively, that fits together and handles new cases, that may implement further inquiry and invention. Candidates, verbal or nonverbal, for new adoption along the way are not asked for their origins or credentials; they may come from hard study, shrewd hunches, or wild guesses. The test is whether they can be made to fit and work. And what works for a time is not expected to work forever or everywhere; nor is even a successful construction taken to preclude alternatives. Overall, advancement of the understanding is rather more like carpentry than computation.

About now someone may want to protest that we cannot so brusquely dispense with the pursuit of truth and knowledge, and ask: "Don't you claim or at least hope that what you are saying is true? And if advancement of understanding involves progress in distinguishing what is right from what is wrong, doesn't that

4. Compare this reconception with that in Paul A. Kolers and Henry L. Roediger III, "Procedures of Mind", *Journal of Verbal Learning and Verbal Behavior*, 23 (1984) 425–449; for instance (p. 425): "The prevailing metaphor for studies of learning and memory emphasizes the acquisition, storage, and retrieval of 'information'. . . Mind is described [in the present paper] in terms of skill in manipulating symbols and the notion of skills is shown to provide a useful framework for accounting for significant aspects of cognitive processes."

involve *knowing* what is right?" To the first question, we answer that we hope what we have been saying may, at least in part, be *right* or somewhere near right, but not that it be true except where truth is required for rightness. Where truth and rightness are at odds, then, like the scientist seeking to formulate effective laws, we choose rightness. And even where truth *is* wanted, that is not transcendent truth concerning the beyond, but immanent truth concerning what the version under consideration makes and refers to. As for the second question, the advancement of understanding does involve progress in distinguishing what is right but *not in knowing* what is right. To determine skillfully and intelligently, but fallibly, whether something is right (or is red, or is dangerous) is not to have a true, certain, and justified belief that it is right (or is red, or is dangerous), whatever that might mean. To the question "How do you know what is right?" our answer is that we don't know that or anything else. The known is unknown.

We work *from* a perspective that takes in the arts, the sciences, philosophy, perception, and our everyday worlds, and *toward* better understanding of each through significant comparison with the others. Speaking schematically, the *first* phase of this effort begins by observing that the use—that is, the fabrication, application, and interpretation—of symbols is centrally involved in all these fields. Accordingly, a general theory of symbols and their functions is outlined (*LA; RR*). The *second* phase confronts the consequences of recognizing that symbols are not merely devices for describing objects, events, a world waiting to be discovered, but enter into the very constitution of what is referred to (*WW*). The present *third* phase starts from the realization that the prevailing conception of philosophy is hopelessly deficient when all fields of cognition, symbols of all kinds, and all ways of referring are taken into account, and so goes on to a search for more comprehensive and responsive concepts.[5]

5. Note, however, that the present third phase does not require agreement with all views set forth in the earlier two phases.

6. Prospects

Such a reconception calls for many modifications other than those we have mentioned. When truth, certainty, and knowledge—all confined to declarative symbols—are supplanted by rightness, adoption, and understanding, some further notions must be stretched to cover or be supplemented or replaced by others that cover the same wider range. Belief, doubt, evidence, probability, confirmation, for example, commonly have to do solely with what statements *say*; we do not, in ordinary discourse, give evidence for or against, or confirm or disconfirm, a way of seeing or a scheme of classification. But success or failure in making such a way or scheme, or any other nonstatement, fit and work when adopted may well be said in a broader sense to confirm or disconfirm it—that is, to render the tenure of its adoption more or less firm. Likewise, though a painting or a piano sonata cannot be proved or disproved, it may 'convince' to the extent that the perceptions or patterns or whatever else it exemplifies or expresses or otherwise refers to, or the way it effects such reference, enhance our understanding—to the extent, in other words, that it is successfully incorporated into our efforts at construction of a version or vision.

Even elementary logical notions raise intriguing problems. The negate of a false statement is true, but the negate of what is wrong may also be wrong; "$2 + 2 = 4$" and "$2 + 2 \neq 4$" are equally wrong answers to some questions. And if a design or rhythm or color or juxtapostion of colors is wrong, is its negate always right? That obviously depends upon how "negate" is to be used in such cases. Is black the negate of all colors, or is the negate of a color its complementary, or since no two colors can occupy the same space at the same time, is every color a negate of every other? Can a style be the negate of another, or only different from it? For nonverbal cases where we have no identified signs or words or phrases for effecting negation, we need some more general notion of *opposition*, probably having several species, some of them parallel to verbal contradiction and contrariety. Logical concepts other than negation—for example, consequence and consistency—will need work of the same kind. Unlike terminal skepticism and irresponsible relativism, constructionalism always has plenty to do.

(*Goodman/Elgin*)

Other Appearances

Versions of the following chapters have been previously published:

Chapter II in *Das Abenteuer der Ideen: Architektur und Philosophie seit der Industriellen Revolution,* ed. Claus Baldus und Vittorio Lampugnani, Berlin: Internationale Bauaustellung, 1987, in German; in *Critical Inquiry* 11 (1985); in *Domus* (May, 1986), in Italian and in English.

Chapter III in *Critical Inquiry* 12 (1986).

Chapter VII (under the title, "Representation, Comprehension, and Competence") in *Social Research* 51 (1984).

Versions of the following chapters are forthcoming:

Chapter I (under the title "Savoir et Faire") in *Encyclopédie Philosophique,* Paris: Presses Univèrsitaires de France, in French.

Chapter IV in *Essays in the Philosophy of Music,* ed. V. Rantala, L. Rowell, and E. Tarasti, Helsinki: Acta Philosophica Fennica, 1987.

Chapter V (under the title, "Pictures in the Mind?") in *Images and Understanding,* ed. H. B. Barlow, Colin Blakemore, and Miranda Westin-Smith, Cambridge University Press.

Chapter VI (under the title "'Just the Facts, Ma'am'!") in *Relativism: Interpretation and Confrontation*, ed. Michael Krausz, Notre Dame: University of Notre Dame Press.

Chapter IX in *Synthese*.

Chapter X in *Bewusstsein, Sprache und die Kunst*, ed. Michael Benedikt, in German.

Name Index

Subject Index